KIDS' BOOK OF
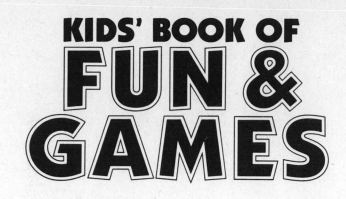

FUN &
GAMES

RUDI McTOOTS
KIDS' BOOK OF
FUN &
GAMES

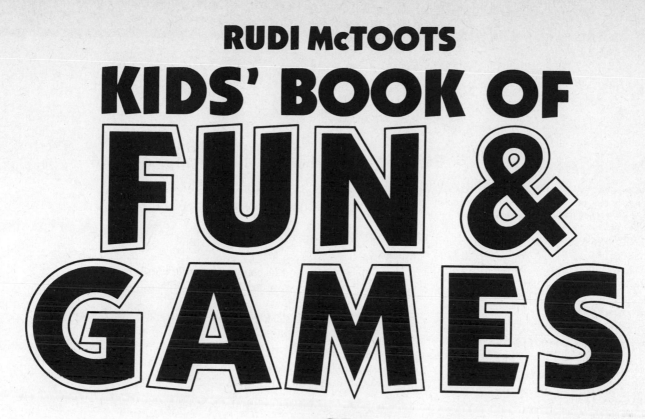

Dreadnaught
Toronto

Created, designed and published at
Dreadnaught
46 Harbord Street
Toronto Canada M5S 1G2

Typesetting: Fleet Typographers Limited, Toronto
Printing: Trigraphic Printing Limited, Ottawa

Distributed in Canada by
Firefly Books Ltd.
3520 Pharmacy Avenue
Scarborough, Ontario M1W 2T8

Published with the assistance of the Canada Council and the Ontario Arts Council

Canadian Cataloguing in Publication Data

McToots, Rudi, 1957-
 Kids' Book of Fun & Games

ISBN 0-919567-26-6

1. Indoor games – Juvenile literature.
2. Amusements – Juvenile literature. I. Title.

GV1203.M28 1984   j793'.01'922   C84-099602-0

CONTENTS

INTRODUCTION

Stuck inside with nothing to do?

Whether its a rainy day, you're on a school trip, babysitting, in class, traveling or sick in bed, being bored is no fun!

If you've already vacuumed the bathtub and polished your comics you can always balance furniture on your chin or give your goldfish breakdancing lessons.

But best of all, you can look through the hundreds of fun ideas in this book. Alone or with friends, you can play great games, make neat things, learn amazing magic tricks and color the pictures.

So why sit around watching old 'Cooking with Madame Fifi' reruns when you can be exploring the hours of fun to be found in these pages!

WHY KNOT?

Stringing Along

Where would we be today without string and all its relatives? Imagine a cowboy without his lasso, or a sailboat without its rigging, or a weaver without thread or a granny without her knitting wool!

Fishermen would be lineless and netless, guitar and violin players would be stringless, birthday presents would be ribbonless and Tarzan would be vineless! A world without string would be pretty dismal!

GNUH!*

Humans have been fascinated with cordage and knots since the days when the first caveperson was crouched in a cave looking for uses for those new thumbs. While fiddling with a long strip of animal skin, the first knot was born.

*TRANSLATION: "QUICK! SOMEBODY INVENT SCISSORS!"

Since that time, string and rope have been used to make anything from snares, weapons and cloth, to buildings and bridges.

AUTO-KNIT

They have also been used to create art; in religious and magic ceremonies; as a Navaho secret 'handshake'; for mathematical calculations and counting; for making poems and telling stories; and for keeping track of the movements of the stars and planets.

Explorers found that they could talk with natives all over the world using string figures. In fact, no modern expedition sets out without taking along an expert on string figures.

Anthropologists are baffled by the fact that string figures, like the ones in this book, are the same around the globe. I don't know if you've ever seen a baffled anthropologist, but it's not a pretty sight.

Now that you know a little more about the exciting family history of string, maybe you'll treat it with respect. After all, you couldn't lace your sneakers without it!

STILL FEELS A BIT LOOSE...

Cutting String Without Scissors

This is an old story about a neat guy named Alexander the Great who lived about 2300 years ago (356 to 323 B.C.)

THAT'S ME

It seems that this big, complicated knot called the **Gordian Knot** (after its creator, King Gordius) had been kicking around for a long time.

JUST A FEW MORE HALF-HITCHES AND A SHEEPSHANK OR TWO

Rumor had it that whoever could untie the knot would rule all of Asia!

WHAT KNOTS!!

Now over the years, many so-called experts tackled the thing, but not one of them made so much as a dent in it...

I WILL RULE!

NO ME! ME!

POWER HUNGRY FOOL

Eventually, our hero heard about this tough knot and couldn't resist going to take a crack at it.

GET OUT OF MY LIGHT AND GO UNTIE THE GORDIAN KNOT WHY DONTCHA!

FUNNY PAPYRUS

G-GOLLY!

He took one look at the knot that had baffled everyone for so long, and then whacked it in half with his trusty sword...

IT IS **THUS** I PERFORM THE TASK!

YIPE

TWAIN

Oh people complained all right, but it was too late. Besides, Alexander fulfilled the prophecy, for he ruled a vast empire of his own making that included Egypt, Greece and Persia.

EGYPT AFRICA

ALEXANDER LAND

CHINA

INDIA

If you don't have a sword or even a pair of scissors handy, this trick is useful for breaking a tough string: Wrap this smart-alec string around your left hand as shown. Close your hand and pull hard on the palm string. It should break at the point where it crosses the other string, if not, keep trying! If you still can't break it, you might as well forget about ever ruling all of Asia!

1.

PALM STRING

2.

Three-strand Solid Braid

This type of braiding works best with flat cord or flat plastic or leather strips, like the kind used in leather work. But almost any kind of string, yarn, twine or shoelace will do. It is nice with strands of different colors, and they make it easier to see what you're doing.

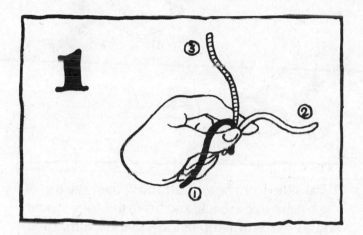

1 Start by tying your three strands in a knot at one end to hold them together. If you are right-handed, the strands are held in the left hand as shown, and the braid is built up from the bottom to the top.

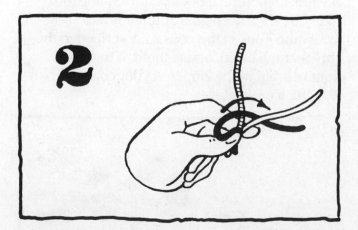

2 Bring strand 1 from the front over to the right and put it between strands 2 and 3. But leave a small loop, which you hold with your thumb as in the picture.

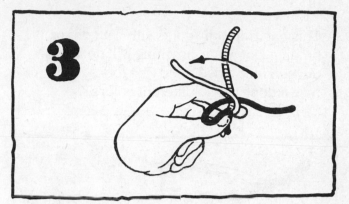

3 Bring strand 2 to the left over strand 1.

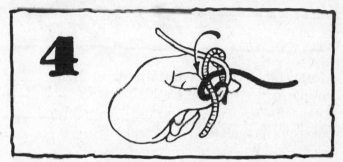

4 Bring strand 3 to the front over strand 2, and push it through the loop you left in strand 1. Tighten the strands.

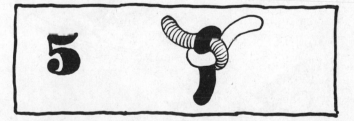

5 You should now have a triangular knot like the one in picture 5.

6 Continue the operation the same way, this time using strand 3 to start off instead of strand 1, as it is the one at the front now. The strands will keep turning, so on the next round you will start off with strand 2, then with strand 1 again, and so on.

7 When the braid is as long as you want it, cut off the loose ends, leaving about half an inch or so. Bend these ends down, and with a pen point push them into the braid under the last row.

Four-strand Square Braid

This one is usually done with flat cord or binding, but again, anything will do. It produces a four-sided braid that looks really nice if done in two different colors.

1 Start off by crossing the strands at their middles.
2 Pass the front strand, strand 1, over strand 2, but leave a small loop in strand 1.

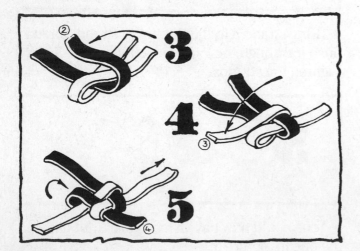

3 Pass strand 2 over strand 1 so that it lies between strand 3 and strand 4.
4 Bring the back strand, strand 3, over strand 2 so that it lies between strand 4 and the little loop you left in strand 1.
5 Now bring strand 4 over strand 3 and push it into the loop in strand 1. Pull all the strands tight.
6 You should get a square knot that looks like picture 6.

7 Pass the front strand, strand 3, over the top of the square to the back, and bring the back strand, strand 1, over the top of the square toward the front.
8 Bring strand 2 from the left and pass it over strand 3 and under strand 1. Bring strand 4 from the right and pass it over strand 1 and under strand 3.
9 Look at picture 9. Does your braiding look like this? If so, keep going until it is as long as you want. Tuck in the ends as described in the three-strand braid, or use them to tie your square braid to the zipper of your coat, to your key chain or whatever.

Five-strand Sennit

This braid is a little harder to learn, but the finished braid is very beautiful, especially if you use colored strands. So if you're in the mood for something a little harder, this is the one to try. The end result is worth it. It produces a wide flat braid that can be used for book marks, belts, hat bands, carrying straps or bracelets. If you want to keep *really* busy, you could even sew a few lengths of braid together to make a handbag, a glasses case or pencil case or almost anything right up to a blanket for an elephant!

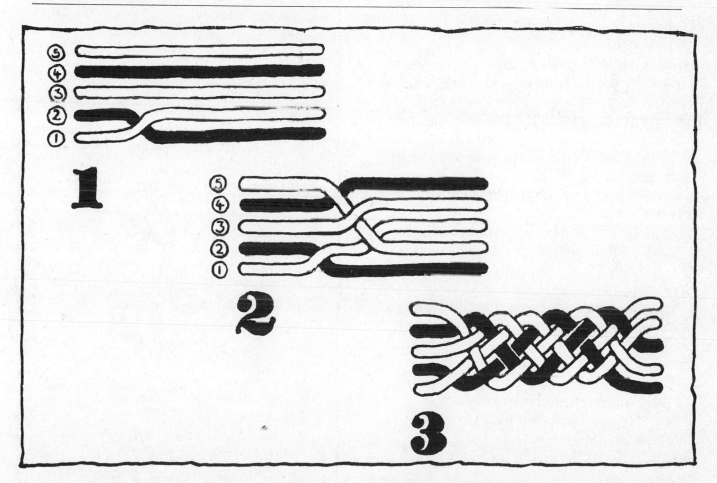

1 Start by bringing the far left strand, strand 1, over strand 2 so that it lies between strand 2 and strand 3.

2 Next pass the far right strand, strand 5, over strand 4, under strand 3 and over strand 1. Strand 5 should now lie between strand 1 and strand 2.

3 Repeat the steps above, bringing the far left strand (now strand 2) over the strand to its right, then the far right strand (now strand 4) over, under and over the three strands to its left. The final braid should look like the last picture.

4 The ends can be tucked back into the braid, left loose, sewn together or tied into a knot. If the band is being formed into a loop, simply tie each strand to its opposite strand at the other end of the braid.

If you have tried all these braids, why not see if you can invent some new one-to-eight strand braids.

Breakfast Escapes

There is an exciting story that goes with this one, but you'll have to learn the trick first. Study the drawings, and the directions will seem as clear as glass. (The transparent kind, that is.) All you need is a piece of string about four feet long with the ends tied together.

1 Hold your left hand with the fingers pointing straight up and the palm toward the right. Grasp the loop of string three inches down from the end with the right hand. Put the little finger of your left hand through the small loop and give the string a half-turn counterclockwise with the right hand.

2 Put the ring finger through the loop formed between the twist in the string and the right hand. Give the string a half-turn, this time clockwise.

3 Then put the middle finger through the small loop and give the string a half-turn counterclockwise.

4 Next put your index finger through the loop in the same way, and give the string a *full turn* clockwise in between the index finger and the thumb.

5 Put the thumb in the loop and give the string another half-turn counterclockwise.

6 Bring the loop back over the thumb, and give the string a half-turn clockwise between the thumb and index finger. Put the index finger in the loop.

7 Give the string a half-turn counterclockwise, and insert the middle finger in the loop. Continue giving half-turns in the opposite direction (clockwise, then counter), and insert the ring and little fingers. Your left hand should now be thoroughly tied up as in the last drawing.

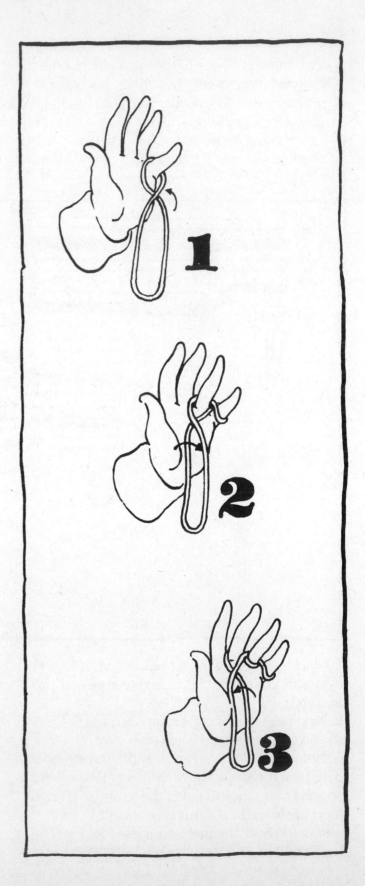

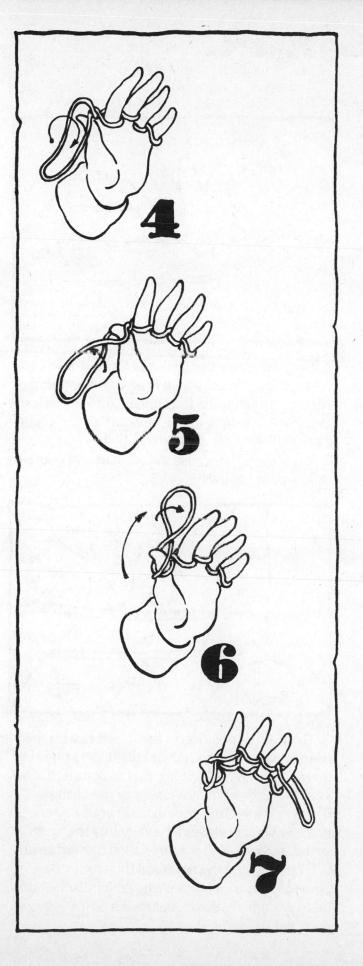

8 If you've done everything right, then when you pull your thumb out of its loops and pull on the string with the right hand, all the loops twisted around the other fingers will seem to melt through the fingers, and the string will fall off your hand. After you've practiced this a bit in private and can do the twisty-turny part easily, begin telling this story to your friends:

Five explorers (you say) set out exploring as explorers often will do. They wandered into the jungle on the isle of Glup-Gup and were captured by a band of wild cannibals. Now, since the Glup-Gupians had just eaten several plump missionaries, they decided to save the explorers until the morning, and then have them hot, with milk and sugar, for breakfast. So they tied them up with one long loop of rope like this…(at this point in the story you wind the string around your fingers as described above). And then they tied the rope to a post…(now give the string to someone to hold tight, or loop it over your foot or something solid like that). The cannibals were by now very tired, so they all went to sleep.

One of the explorers had been a Boy Scout and managed to slip out of the knotty ropes during the night, as the cannibals snored in their beds…(pull your thumb out of its loops). He freed the rest of the explorers and they ran off to their boat…(pull the left hand quickly and the string will fall off)!

In the morning the hungry cannibals found that breakfast had run off in the night, leaving the end of the rope still tied to the post!

This also makes a great magic trick, especially if you tell your audience that you are going to cut your fingers off with string. Give the long end to someone, telling him to pull hard on the count of three. As he pulls, bend your thumb forward and the string quickly slips off and seems to cut through your fingers like a knife through butter! Make sure you practice the tying part thoroughly before you try this, or your fingers might *really* fall off!

Some String Figures

String figures are common to folks all over the world. Eskimos, Indians, South Sea natives, Africans, Asians and Orientals can all show you string pictures of things from their daily lives. Often there is a story or chant that goes with the figure, and people from different cultures can even 'talk' with string!

It's very difficult to describe string figures on paper. The instructions may look complicated, but in fact the figures are easy to do, so don't give up. Having someone else read the steps aloud may make it easier. All the tangles and curses of your first tries will be worth it when you finally see the string picture appear magically between your hands.

When you know these figures, you can find books on more string figures, or you can even invent some new ones!

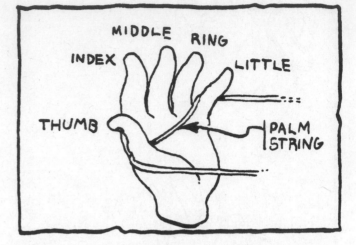

2 The fingers are described as 'thumb' (which is obvious); 'index,' which is next to the thumb; 'middle,' which is the long one next to the index; 'ring,' which is next in line, and 'little' – which is that small pinky at the end.
3 Any strings that cross the palm are, of course, called 'palm' strings.

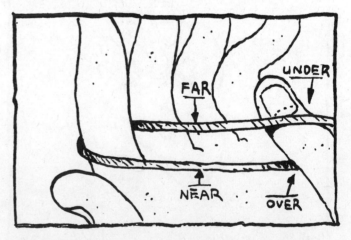

4 The normal position of the hands is with the palms toward each other and the fingers pointing up (as in opening A). It is usual to return to this position after each movement of the strings.
5 Of each loop that goes around your fingers, there is a string closer to you, called the 'near' string, and one farther away, called the 'far' string.
6 When making the figures, a finger may be passed *over* or *under* a string. You must be careful to get this right and make sure that the loops don't get twisted!

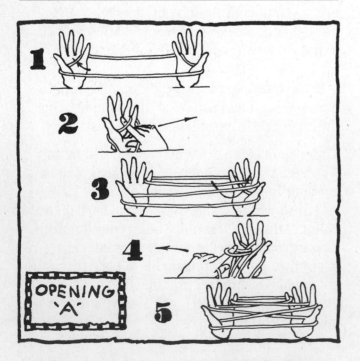

1 Before you leap into action, study the first set of drawings. These show how to make 'opening A,' which most string figures start with.

A String Boy Climbs a String Palm Tree

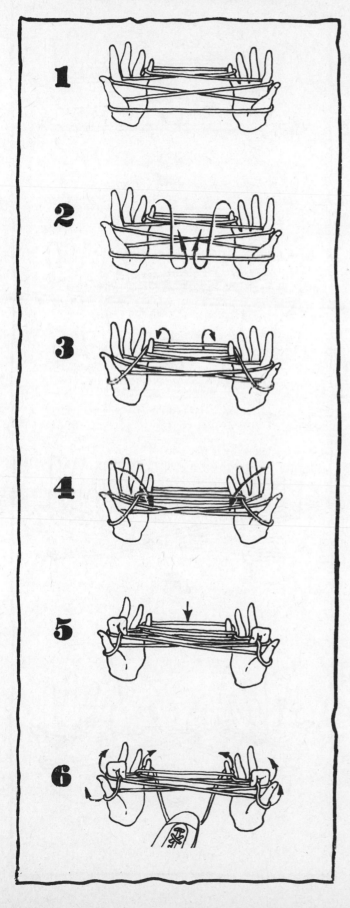

This is one of the easiest string figures and yet one of the most dramatic and exciting.

1 Start with opening A.

2 Next bring the little fingers toward you, over the index-finger loops and the far thumb string, and put them into the thumb loop from above. Pick up the near thumb string on the backs of the little fingers, and return the fingers to their first position, leaving the string on the thumbs.

3 With the thumb and index finger of each hand, lift the first far string off the little fingers, passing it over the loops just picked up, which stay in place. You must be careful while doing this that you don't lose the strings on the other fingers.

4 Bend the index fingers down into their loops. When you do this you should push the string that crosses the index-finger loops against the palm with the tip of the index fingers.

5 With your foot or a book, firmly hold down the far little-finger string.

6 Release all the finger and thumb strings *except* those held by the index fingers against the palms. Shake the strings so that the loops are untangled from each other.

7 Pull up a little on the left loop, then the right loop, and so on, and the boy will shinny up the tree.

8 As he gets higher, he gets smaller and smaller until all that is left is a palm tree with a bunch of coconuts in the center.

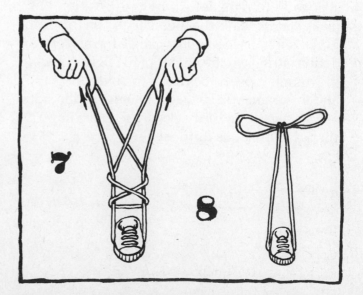

The Two Headhunters

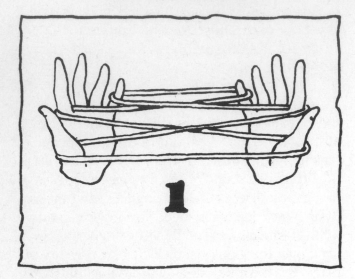

1

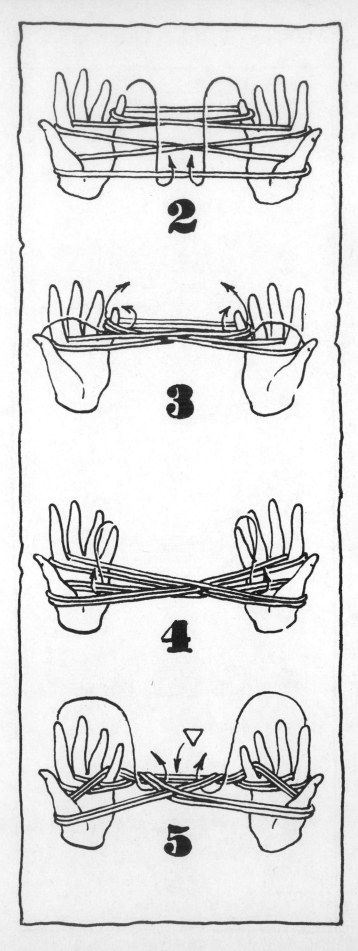

1 Start with opening A.

2 Bend the little fingers toward you, over all the strings except the near thumb string, and down into the thumb loop. Pick up the near thumb string with the backs of the little fingers and lift it clear of the thumbs, returning the little fingers to their first position.

3 You should now have one loop on each index finger and two loops on each little finger. Move the thumbs away from you and *under* the index loop. Pick up from below, with the thumbs, the two near little-finger strings and return the thumbs to their original position, releasing the little-finger loops from the little fingers.

4 Bend the little fingers toward you over the index loop, and take up from below (on the backs of the little fingers) the two far thumb strings. Return the little fingers to position, but make sure to leave the thumb loops on this time!

5 You should see a small triangle formed of double strings in the center of the figure near the thumbs. Insert the tips of the index fingers into this triangle from below. Pulling out the sides of the triangle on the backs of the index fingers, spread your hands further apart.

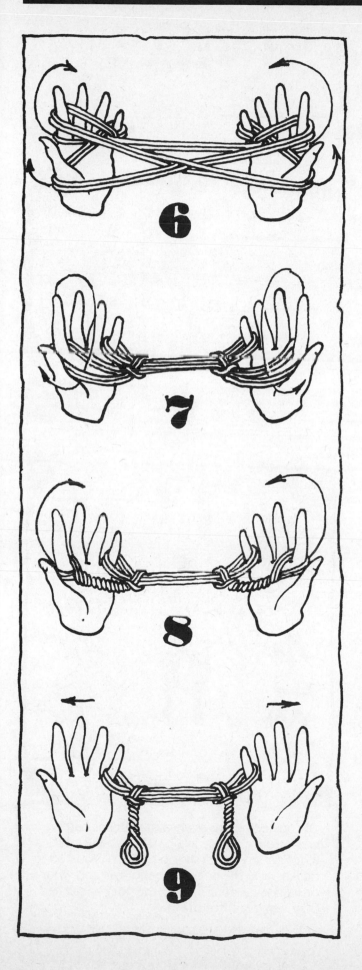

6 Keep a firm hold on all the strings. Reach across with the right hand, and with the right thumb and index finger lift the lower single loop on the left index finger up over the other two index loops and off the tip of the finger, letting it fall between your hands. Now reach across with the left hand and do the same thing with the lower single loop on the right index finger. Then release the loops from the thumbs.

7 Now, by twisting the index fingers away from you (this is called 'navahoing') you should be able to twist the string around two or three times, the more the better. If you can't do this, don't worry. Just remove the loops from the index fingers (one finger at a time!) and twist them (the loops, not the fingers) around three or four times.

8 Remove the twisted loops from the index fingers if they are not off already, and let the loops hang down. If you are using very stiff string, the loops might be convinced to stand up, making them more lifelike, for these loops are the headhunters.

9 If you pull on the left little-finger strings, the two savage hunters will charge at each other.

10 When they meet, they bash at each other until either they both kill each other and disappear, or one kills the other and walks off with the head. You have to see it to believe it!

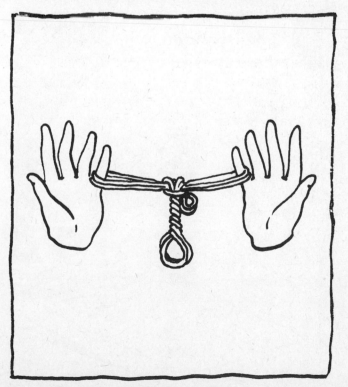

RIP AND WRINKLE

Paper Play

If you were in China 2000 years ago, you would have had to wait about 150 years for a guy called T'sai Lun to invent paper before you could play these paper games.

IT'S ABOUT TIME...

INVENTIONS WHILE -U- WAIT

The Egyptians couldn't wait, so thousands of years earlier they thought up papyrus, a writing material made from a certain kind of reed. Papyrus didn't fold at all, but it was easier to write on than stone, which doesn't fold too well either.

TRY ROLLING IT...

MILK EGGS T.P.

Of course, there was always vellum or parchment around to use in a pinch. If you wanted to jot down a quick shopping list, all you had to do was grab the nearest goat or calf and write on its skin, preferably after the goat or calf had been removed from it.

The ancient Japanese made their paper from the inner bark of the mulberry tree and believed that paper was a god, so of course cutting it was considered a sin, if not downright disrespectful!

Nature, always slightly ahead of its time, had been making paper long before the Dawn of Man. In fact, one version goes as far back as the Dawn of Wasps, and even today you can still see paper wasp nests hanging in trees or under eaves.

The first honest-to-goodness manmade paper was manufactured from the inner bark of trees and rags. Centuries later, someone was watching a wasp at work, and realized that paper could also be made from the wood of the tree, which is what most paper today is made from.

The paper play in this chapter is fun no matter what kind of paper you use! Grab a few sheets and maybe a pencil or two, and read on . . . .

Origami

Origami is the Japanese name for the art of paper folding. There are hundreds of things that can be made by folding paper, and origami fans (there are lots!) are always finding new ones. After trying these, see if you can invent some of your own.

The next four paper figures are each made from a square of paper. If you only have rectangular sheets, here's how to make squares from them:

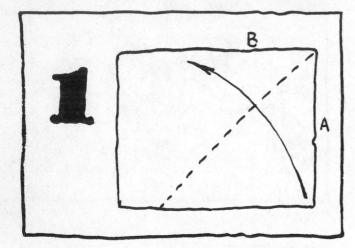

1 Bring the bottom right-hand corner up, making sure that the right-hand edge of the sheet (A) lies exactly along the top edge (B).

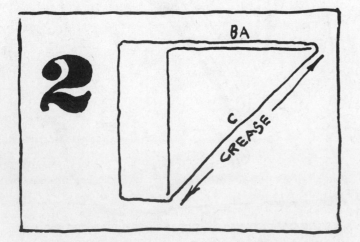

2 Once you have lined up the two edges, crease the fold (C) with your finger.

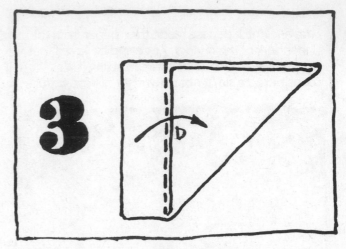

3 Fold the part that sticks out beyond the edge (D) over that edge, and crease it with your finger.

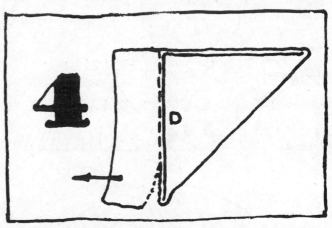

4 Fold this part back again, and cut or tear along the crease.

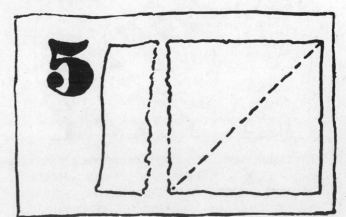

5 Unfold the sheet of paper, and you will see that it is a square.

Paper Cup

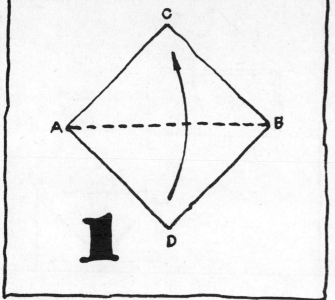

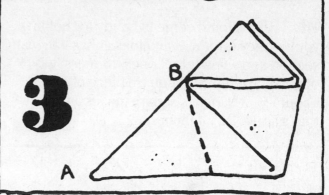

1 You need a square piece of paper (shiny or wax paper is best) about nine inches long by nine wide. Fold corner D up to meet corner C, creasing along fold AB.

3 Turn the paper over. Fold A over as you folded B, so that it looks like picture 4.

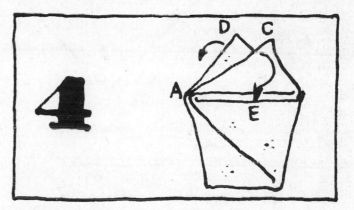

4 The two triangular flaps at the top (C and D) should be folded down away from each other and tucked under on each side at E.

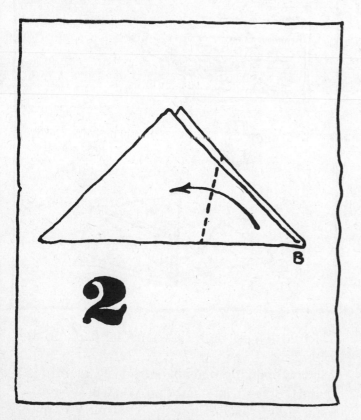

2 It should now look like the second picture. Next fold B over so it looks like picture 3.

5 The almost finished cup should look like this picture. All you have to do to finish it is to open out the top. If you fold the two bottom corners under slightly, the cup will stand on its own.

Wallet

This wallet should come in handy for holding your money or other valuables. It has one main section and a few secret ones for messages or other secret things. A square piece of paper about 8½ or 9 inches square makes a wallet that's about 2 by 4 inches.

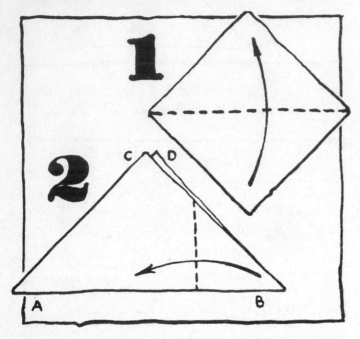

1 Fold the bottom corner up to the top one, like the first fold for the paper cup.
2 Then fold corner B over about two-thirds of the way along the bottom edge, but keep the bottom edge lined up.

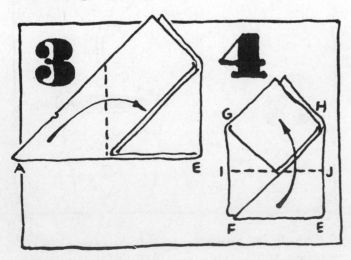

3 Fold corner A over to meet the new corner E, then tuck it under into the folds.
4 Fold the bottom edge EF up to corners GH.

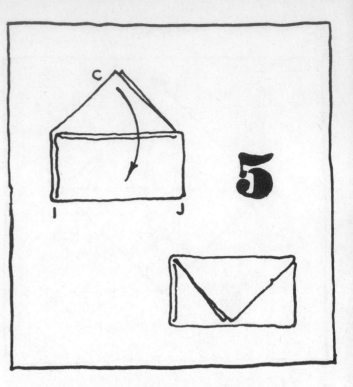

5 Fold the top triangles down to the new bottom edge IJ. Your wallet is now finished.

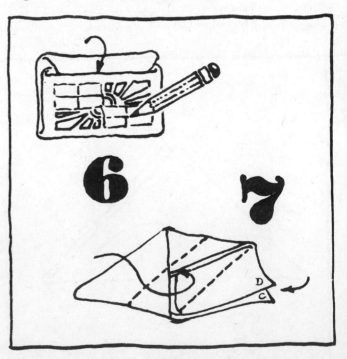

6 To close it up, tuck the triangular flap into the folds.
7 If you open it out again and separate corners D and C of the triangular flap, you will see the main hiding place. There are a few more compartments, which you will have to find for yourself. I can't tell you because they're secret!

Windmill

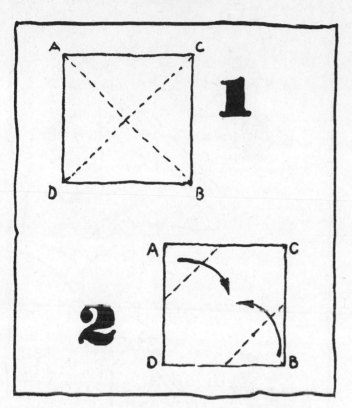

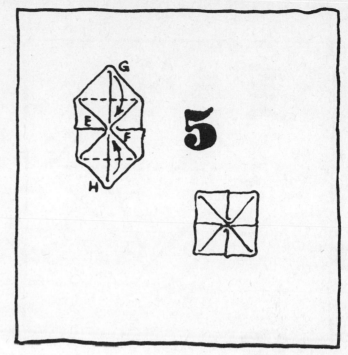

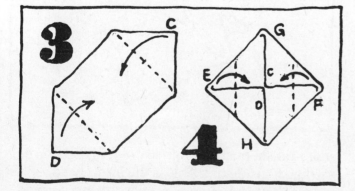

1 Start with a square of paper any size and fold corners A and B together and crease. Unfold again and fold the other two corners, C and D, together. Your square should now have two folds across it from corner to corner, like the one in the first picture.

2 Fold corners A and B in so that they meet in the center where the two folds cross.

3 Turn the paper over and fold corners C and D together so they meet in the middle on the other side.

4 You now have a smaller square. Fold its corners, E and F, together at the center in the same way.

5 Turn the paper over again and repeat the process on the other side with corners G and H. You now have an even smaller square.

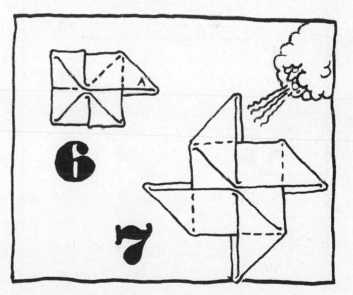

6 Open out the last small triangular flap (H) again, and pull on the corner exposed (A) until it looks like picture 6.

7 Do this with each of the other flaps (E, F and G) and your windmill is complete. Poke the point of a pencil or pen through the center, and thread a string through the hole. Hold the string by both ends, and blow on the windmill. It will spin incredibly fast! You can also use a pin to stick the windmill onto a stick.

Bird

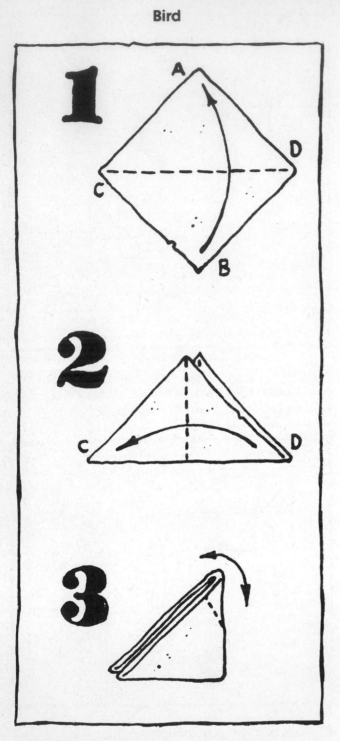

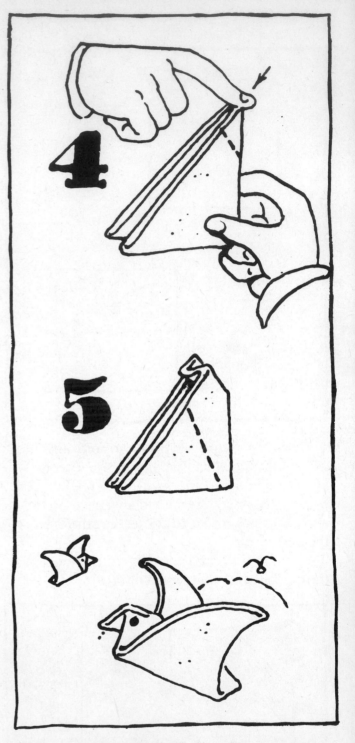

1 Fold a square of paper on the dotted line shown in the first picture, joining corners A and B.
2 Fold this triangle in half, joining corners C and D.
3 Fold the top point along the dotted line as shown in the drawing. Bend it back and forth a few times to loosen the paper, then straighten.
4 Push your thumb in between the two layers of the long side of the triangle and, with your index finger, push the folded point in and down, turning it inside out. This is the bird's head.
5 Fold the two left-hand corners down on opposite sides at the dotted line. These are the wings of the bird. Curve the tips down slightly. If you hold your bird by the tail with your right hand, you can make its wings flap by shaking your hand.

Thinking Caps

Extensive scientific tests and studies have proven beyond a doubt that the best kind of paper to use for thinking caps is a double sheet of newspaper, but any large sheet of paper will work just as well. So much for scientific studies.

Pirate's Hat

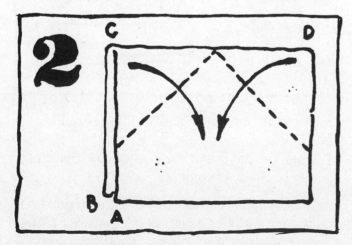

1 Fold a long rectangle of paper in half, folding side A down to meet side B. If you are using a double sheet of newspaper, this fold is already made.

2 Fold the top right and top left corners (C and D) down, as shown in the next drawing.

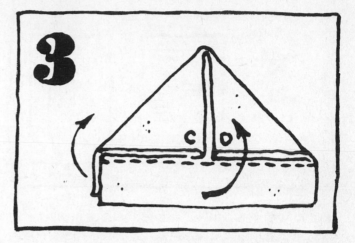

3 You should now have two single-thickness flaps at the bottom. Fold these up on either side.

4 Open the bottom out and the pirate's hat is finished. Shiver me timbers!

Pilot's Cap

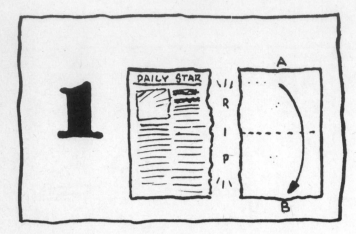

1 You will need only a single sheet of newspaper to make it, instead of a double sheet. Fold the sheet in half, bringing the top edge (A) down to meet the bottom edge (B).

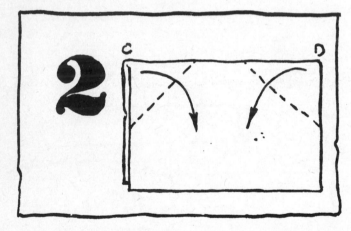

2 Fold the left and right corners (C and D) down, but not all the way down. See the picture.

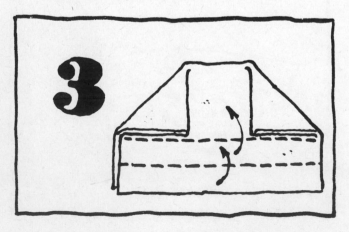

3 Fold the front flap up halfway, then fold it the rest of the way up.

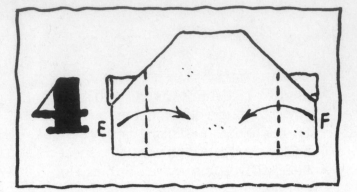

4 Turn the paper over and fold the left and right edges (E and F) over at the dotted lines. The left and right edges should *not* meet in the middle.

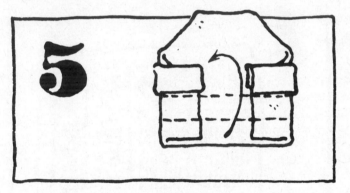

5 Fold the bottom flap up as you did the first one, by folding it halfway and then all the way.

6 Tuck the bottom edge of the flap behind E and F.

7 Open the hat out at the bottom and place at a jaunty angle on your head.

All of these hats can be decorated with paint, cut paper, sparkles, feathers or whatever. Using these patterns for practice, it shouldn't be too hard to design and invent some of your own paper hats.

Printer's Cap

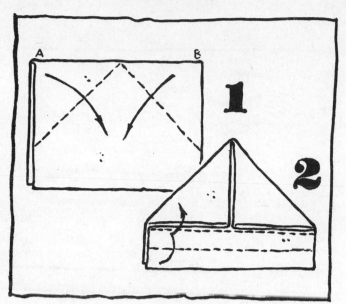

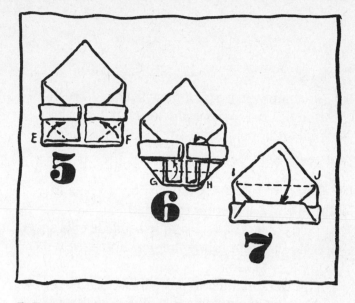

1 It starts off just like the pirate's hat, with a large rectangular sheet folded in half and the top left and right corners folded down.
2 Don't fold the bottom flap all the way up. Instead, fold it halfway up, and then fold it up again, as the second picture shows.

5 Fold corners E and F up as shown.
6 Fold the bottom flap in half as shown. Unfold the flap again, and this time fold the whole flap up and tuck the end GH in behind.
7 Fold the top triangle down at IJ and tuck the point in behind as well.

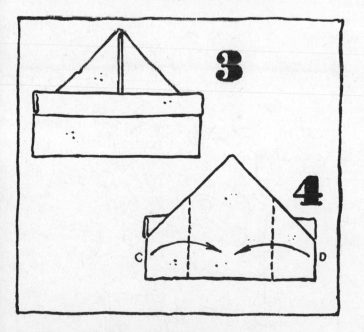

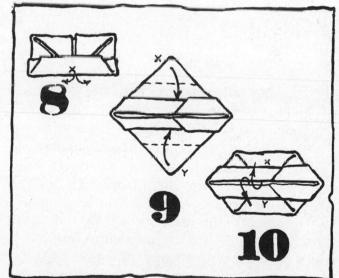

3 It should now look like the third picture. Don't fold up the second flap yet.
4 Turn your hat-to-be over. Fold the left and right ends (C and D) in on the dotted lines, so that they meet in the middle, as shown in the drawing.

8 Insert your thumbs in the bottom at point X and open out *all the way.*
9 Flatten it out a bit and it should look like picture 9. Fold the top corners, X and Y, down to the middle and tuck them under the bands.
10 Open it out at the middle and it is ready to wear – whether you are a printer, a thinker, or you just have a cold scalp!

Scribbles

PLAYERS:
ANY NUMBER

You can't win any points with this game, but that doesn't make it any less fun. It can be played alone or with any number of players.

1 The object of the game is to turn a simple scribble into a picture of something.
2 Each player draws a simple squiggle on a sheet of paper without lifting the pen, and passes it on to another person.
3 This person must include the squiggle as one of the lines in a drawing of a scene or object of some kind.
4 The pictures make it clear. The thick lines are the original scribbles.

5 If you want, you can make the game harder by making a rule that the finished drawing must be made without lifting the pen.

Sets

PLAYERS:
2 OR MORE

1 On a large sheet of paper write the numbers from one to twenty scattered all over the sheet, and put a small circle around each. Leave as much room as possible around each number.
2 Now write the same numbers again on the same sheet, scattering them around. Make sure that the same numbers are far from each other.
3 The object of this crazy game is to connect each pair of numbers together with a line that does not cross or touch any other line.
4 Each player makes up a sheet, which he passes to the player next to him.
5 The first player to properly complete his sets scores one point and wins the round.

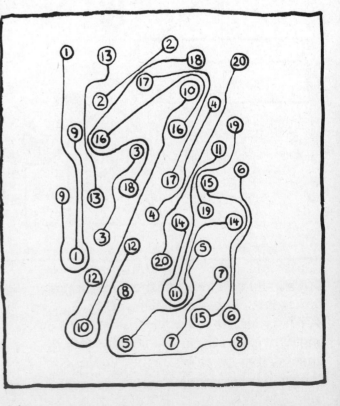

Possibilities

PLAYERS:
2 OR MORE

This has been a favorite game for ages. It was old in the time of Queen Elizabeth I, for what it's worth.

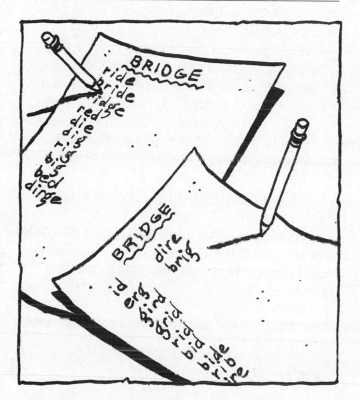

1 In this game players use the letters of a large word to form smaller words.

2 You can't use a letter twice to form a new word unless there are two of them in the first word.

3 For example, let's say you decide on the word 'bridge.' Each player takes a pencil and paper, and keeping his sheets hidden from the other players, starts to write down all the words he can think of, using the letters b, r, i, d, g and e. These are some of the many (more than you would think!) words that can be made from the word bridge: ride, bride, ridge, red, die, dig, rig, big, bed, dirge, id, erg, gird, grid, rid, bid, bide, rib, ire, dire, brig…the list goes on. Do you see any that I've missed?

4 The winner is the player with the most real words made from the original.

Connections

PLAYERS:
2 OR MORE

To play this exciting game you need to be sharp and alert! On your toes! You have to have the eye of an artist, the hand of a brain surgeon, the mind of a chess champion and a pencil and paper.

1 Draw an even square grid of dots, any number to a side, like the one in this drawing.

2 Players take turns drawing one straight, short line between two dots that are side by side (no diagonal lines).

3 The object of the game is to complete as many squares as you can, and to prevent the other players from doing the same thing.

4 When you complete a square, you put your initial in it and take an extra turn. If you finish another square, you take another turn, etc. If you make two boxes by adding one line, you get only one extra turn.

5 When all the dots are used up, count up the number of squares each player has initialed to find the winner. The player with the highest score subtracts the next highest score to get his final number of points.

6 Always try to avoid making the third side of a square because that means that the next player can complete the square and put his own initial in it. When you start out this is easy enough to do, but as the game goes on it becomes harder and harder to avoid drawing the third side.

S.O.S.

Like the distress code of the same name, the game S.O.S. is internationally known, and is certainly a lot more fun.

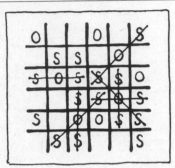

1 Draw a grid a little like a Tic Tac Toe grid, only with a lot more lines – at least five by five. See the drawing.

2 Each player can write either an S *or* an O in any empty square on the grid. The object, as in Tic Tac Toe, is to form three letters in a straight or diagonal line so that they spell out S.O.S. and also to prevent the other players from doing the same thing.

3 Once you have formed an S.O.S., draw a line through it, give yourself one point and move again. Again, you can write an S or an O in any empty square on the board.

4 If two lines of S.O.S. are formed when you put one letter on the grid, you count two points but only get one extra move.

5 Any letter can be used as often as you want to form a line of S.O.S. This means that an S in the center of the grid could have an S.O.S. above it, below it, to the left and right and on each of the four diagonals.

6 When every space on the grid is filled up, the winner is the person with the highest number of S.O.S.s formed.

7 If you see an S.O.S. anywhere on the grid that has been there for a while and is unclaimed, you can claim it and score a point for it, whether you formed it or not.

Memorization

In Rudyard Kipling's great book *Kim*, this game is taught to Kim by one of his employers, an Indian jewel merchant. The merchant teaches it to him using gems and precious stones in order to improve his powers of observation.

1 If you don't have any spare jewels kicking around, you can play this game with an assortment of small objects instead, such as a pen, some coins, a match, etc.

2 If you don't have this many things, have the 'jewel merchant' draw the objects on a sheet of paper.

3 The other players get thirty seconds or one minute to look over the assortment of objects drawn, and then the sheet is covered up. If you don't have a watch, count up to 100.

4 The players must try to write down a list of all the objects they saw on the paper, keeping their lists hidden from each other. If you want, you can set a time limit on this, say two minutes or so.

5 The player with the highest number of objects guessed correctly wins a point and becomes the jewel merchant for the next round.

Hangman

PLAYERS:
2

OOPS! ONE WRONG GUESS TOO MANY!

This game is so old it's ancient, and the only reason it's been around so long is that it's a lot of fun! The rules change slightly from place to place, but the version here seems to be the most widely known. All you need is a sheet (or pad) of paper, a pen or pencil and a pinch of the smarts.

1 The basic idea of the game is this: one player thinks of a word (no names!) and the other player must guess what it is.

2 The first player must give the following hints to make the guessing easier. On the sheet of paper, the first player must put down a small dash for every letter of the word, and then fill in the vowels of the word (a, e, i, o, u) on the dashes where they should go. For example, the word 'hangman' would look like this:

__ a __ __ __ a __

3 Now the second player is ready to start guessing, one letter at a time. If he guesses a letter correctly, the first player must fill in the right dash with the letter guessed. For example, with the word 'hangman,' if the second player guesses *n*, the first player must fill in the third and last dashes, so that the word now looks like this:

__ a n __ __ a n

4 If a wrong guess is made, the first player writes the letter guessed down below (this is so the second player doesn't guess the same letter twice), and he draws the first stroke of the hanged man shown in the picture.

5 Two strokes make the gallows, one stroke the rope, one the head, one for the body and two each for the arms and legs. So in all, the second player can make nine wrong guesses before he is hanged.

6 At any point the second player can make a stab at guessing the whole word, but, if he guesses wrong, two strokes are added to the hanged man.

7 If the whole man is completed before the second player guesses the word, he loses the game, and the first player wins one point.

Here are some hints for guessing:

If there is no *u* in the word, then it stands to reason that there is also no *q*.

If there are few or no vowels in the word, then chances are that there is a *y* in it.

If the third last and second last letters are *i* and *o*, then there is a good chance that the ending of the word is *-tion* or *-sion*.

If the third last letter is *i*, there is a chance that the ending of the word is *-ing*.

Sprouts

PLACERS:
2

This is an amazing game. The rules are so simple that you can learn them in five minutes and remember them always. Yet it's challenging enough that you can play it for hours.

1 Start by putting any number of dots (more than six and less than 15 is best) on a sheet of paper. Leave plenty of space around them.

2 Players take turns at drawing lines, straight or curved, connecting two dots or looping back to the same dot. A new dot is placed anywhere on this new line after it is drawn. In a game of two dots, the first player can make any one of the five moves shown in the drawing.

3 The two basic rules of play are these:

a) The line drawn can be any size or shape, but it can't cross itself or any other line. It should stop at the dots and not pass *through* them.

b) No dot can have more than three lines coming out of it. Each new dot that's drawn on a line already has two lines coming out of it – and only one more can be added before it is 'dead.'

4 The player to make the last legal (that is, following the rules) move is the winner. Watch out for those illegal moves – those which cross lines or use dead dots.

5 In the picture are two sample six-dot games showing some of the beautiful patterns that sprout out of a scattering of dots. Note that even though there are some dots that are not dead (that is, they don't have three lines coming out of them), they cannot be reached without crossing a line, or they have no partner dots to join, so the games are finished.

FINISH
THIS
GAME

Paper Dice

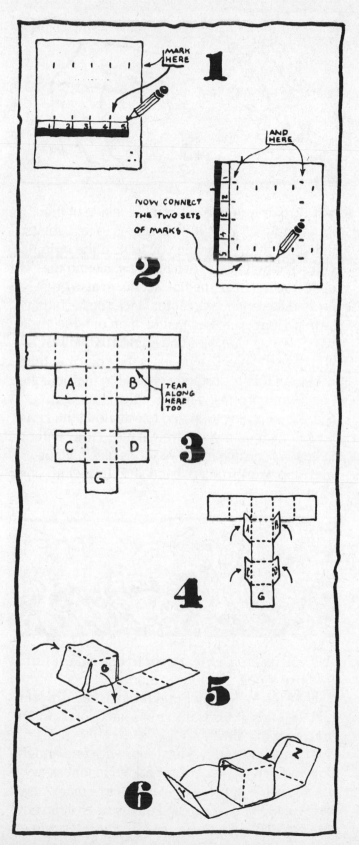

Actually, one dice is called a *die*, so until you make two, this is called a paper die. If you want to use your die, try guessing what each throw will be. You could also invent some funny dice games or look up the dice games at the end of the Scrap Happy chapter, and *get shaking!*

1 Use a ruler to mark off a five-square grid, as shown in the first two pictures. When finished, you should have a perfect square marked off into 25 smaller squares.
2 Using your pencil to thicken the lines, copy the diagram shown in the third picture onto your grid. The thick lines show where to cut, and the dotted ones show where to fold.
3 *Carefully* cut along all thick lines.
4 Fold the side tabs A, B, C and D so that they point straight up.
5 Fold up tab G and continue folding up the middle row of squares until you have a cube sitting in the center of a long strip.
6 Fold up the two ends of the strip (tabs Y and Z) and tuck tabs Y and Z into the slits on each side of the top. You should now have a cube that sits still without flying apart.
7 To change this cube into a die, all that needs to be done is the dotting. The dots on the opposite sides of a die always add up to seven, which means that when you put your dots on, be sure to put the 6 opposite the 1, 5 opposite 2 and 4 opposite 3.

Möbius Madness

Möbius may have been a mad mathematician, but since his discovery of the strip that bears his name, things have never been quite the same. Who would have thought that by giving a long strip of paper a twist or two and forming a loop, you would be making something capable of antics beyond your wildest imaginings? Mathematicians get tickled positively pink when you give them a chance to talk about this comical strip. But the talk is mostly numbers, so let's leave the technical stuff out and just stick to the fun part.

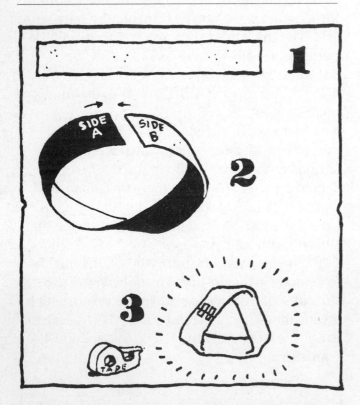

1 Take a strip of paper about two inches wide by a foot or two long.
2 Hold the ends of the strip together so that it forms a big loop, then give one of the ends a half-twist.
3 Join the ends with tape or glue. You are now holding an honest-to-goodness Möbius strip, model A.

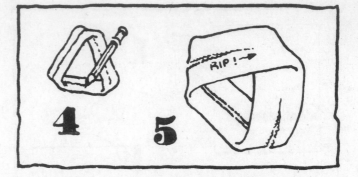

4 Try to draw a line around the inside of the strip with your pencil. This seems to take longer than it should, but when you look at the strip, you see why. Instead of just going around the inside of the strip, the line seems to also go around the outside! In actual fact, the Möbius strip no longer *has* an inside or an outside, it has only one side, and one edge! That half-twist you gave the piece of paper is the culprit in this caper. All this is perfectly natural to mathematicians, but I promised to leave them out of this.
5 Take your new loop and tear it along the center (along the line you drew, if it's in the center). Instead of turning into two loops like any normal loop would, this twisted strip turns into one long loop!

6 If you make your tear over to one side, it turns into two loops, one longer than the other.
7 If you give the paper one *full* twist before you join the ends, it turns into two joined loops when you cut it in half!
8 Try making and tearing loops with one-and-a-half and two twists and, for added madness, try tearing some of these off-center. How many new kinds of Möbius strips can you discover or invent for yourself?

Tri-hexaflexagon

Tri-hexaflexa-*what*!?

If you are baffled now, just wait till you read the explanation of these weird and wonderful inter-dimensional doors. It might help to confuse you to know that a hexaflexagon is a six-sided figure, which is usually folded from a straight strip of paper.

The hexaflexagon we are going to make is called a tri-hexaflexagon because it has three faces, two visible and one hidden. Other hexaflexagons have six, nine, twelve or more faces. When this strange but innocent looking hexagon is 'flexed' (hence the name), the two outside faces change! Messages or designs drawn on one face disappear, only to reappear later, garbled and rearranged, much like this explanation.

Luckily the things are much easier to make than to explain.

To make it, you will need a strip of paper at least one inch wide by ten inches long. When you are cutting the paper to make this strip, be sure that it is exactly the same width all the way along.

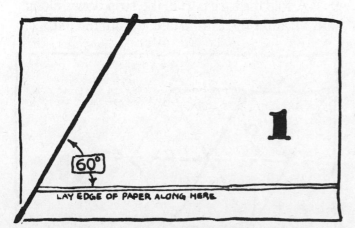

1 The first drawing shows a 60-degree angle, which is the angle you find in all three corners of a triangle with all sides of equal length. These triangles are what hexaflexagons are made of.

2 Lay your strip of paper on the 60-degree angle so that the bottom long side of the strip rests along the double line, and the corner of the strip just touches the corner of the angle.

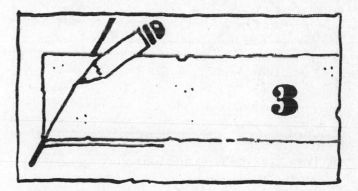

3 With a pencil and a ruler (or anything with a straight edge) join the two ends of the thick line that sticks out on either side of the strip of paper. You now have a 60-degree angle marked off on the left-hand end of your strip.

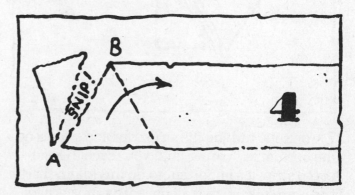

4 Cut along line AB.

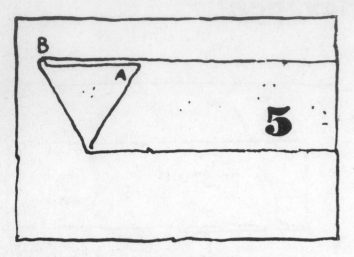

5 Fold up corner A so that it touches the top side and edge AB lies along the top side.

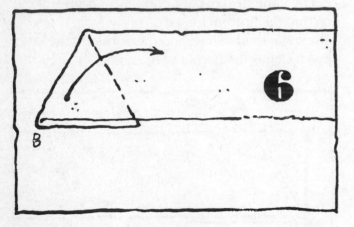

6 Turn over the strip and fold up corner B until it touches the top side.

7 Continue turning the strip over and folding up the bottom left corner until you reach the end of the strip. It's important to do this folding part very carefully, so that all the edges and corners meet exactly.

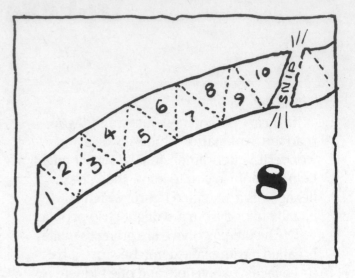

8 Unfold your strip. Count off ten triangles, and tear off the extra ones from the right-hand end.

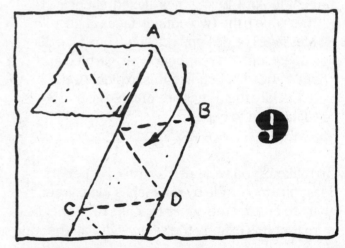

9 Now fold the long part of the strip down, along line AB, after the third triangle from the left.

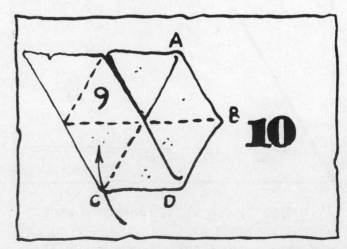

10 Fold the last four triangles up, along line CD.

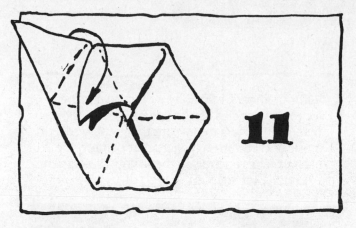

11 The second last triangle, number nine, is lying over the first triangle. Pull the first one out so that it now lies over nine.

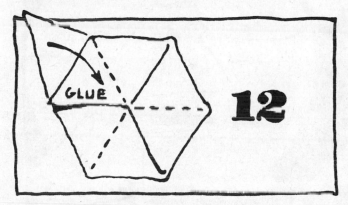

12 Fold the last triangle over on top of the first and stick it down with glue.

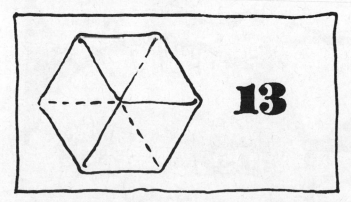

13 You are now the proud owner of a tri-hexaflexagon. You can see that it has six sides and two visible faces (one face is hidden). Decorate the two faces with geometrical designs. You may be wondering why you went to all the trouble of folding the dad-blasted thing, when all it does is lie there with a smug look on its faces. Read on.

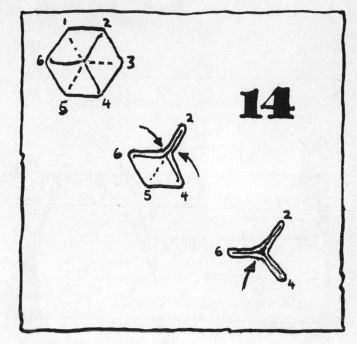

14 To make the little critter spring into action, you merely bring every *second* corner up together to a point.

This part is easier to figure out if you number the corners of one face from 1 to 6. Lay the hexaflexagon flat and bring corners 1 and 3 together until they touch. Then bring corner 5 up to the other two. Turn the figure over, and open out the other face by pushing the point with your finger. If the point *won't* open, don't worry. You have formed a 'node.' All you have to do is open the tri-hexaflexagon again and bring corners 2, 4 and 6 together, instead of 1, 3 and 5.

You may have noticed that your hexaflexagon looks a lot like a flattened Möbius strip. That's because it *is* a flattened Möbius strip! You could put your pencil on it and run a line all the way around and back to your starting point, and it would cover all sides.

Be careful that you don't lose your pencil in it, because hexaflexagons are a little like Alice's looking glass. They are doors to other worlds and dimensions. Anything idly dropped or dripped into a hexaflexagon may just end up in someone's lap in the fourth dimension!

Try inventing some of your own hexaflexagons – can you make one with more hidden faces? Do different shapes than triangles work?

FOR FINGERS

Digital Play

All those poor animals out there with no fingers must envy us humans, because fingers can handle anything from chopping bricks karate-style to the most delicate brain surgery.

Without fingers, humanity would be another forgotten species. It was fingers that built the pyramids, fingers that wrote the great works of music and literature, fingers that painted the masterpieces and raised the mighty skyscrapers. And don't let any foot tell you otherwise.

Besides being helpful, fun and musical, our digits are intelligent too. Our ten fingers are the basis for our entire number and counting system.

Fingers can talk too. Hearing-impaired people use a finger alphabet to communicate. North American Indians used to talk with folks from other tribes using hand signs, and Doctor Doolittle would be proud of the psychologists who have taught chimps to talk using sign language.

There are many more examples of fingers being helpful to humans: Little Jack Horner's Thumb Plum, for example, or Sherlock Holmes's Famous Fingerprint Clue, and the Little Dutch Boy's Finger in the Leaking Dyke.

All in all, you must admit that fingers are pretty swell guys. How about treating them to some of the finger fun in this chapter? They will have a chance to perform a couple of corny magic tricks, to act on stage and in the movies, to make friends with other fingers, to play games of chance and skill against each other and to try out their reflexes.

Sound like fun? Okay, all you have to do now is get your fingers to agree to turn the page!

Shadow Play

About a hundred years ago people went to see performers do this kind of thing on stage. With the help of your ever-ready fingers, though, you should be able to see a shadow play right where you are.

If you have a strong light source, such as a patch of sunlight on the wall or a flashlight at night, try out a few of the shadow friends shown here, to brighten things up a bit!

With a whole cast of shady animals and strange-looking people to choose from, you should be able to find a few characters for your play.

Finger Puppets

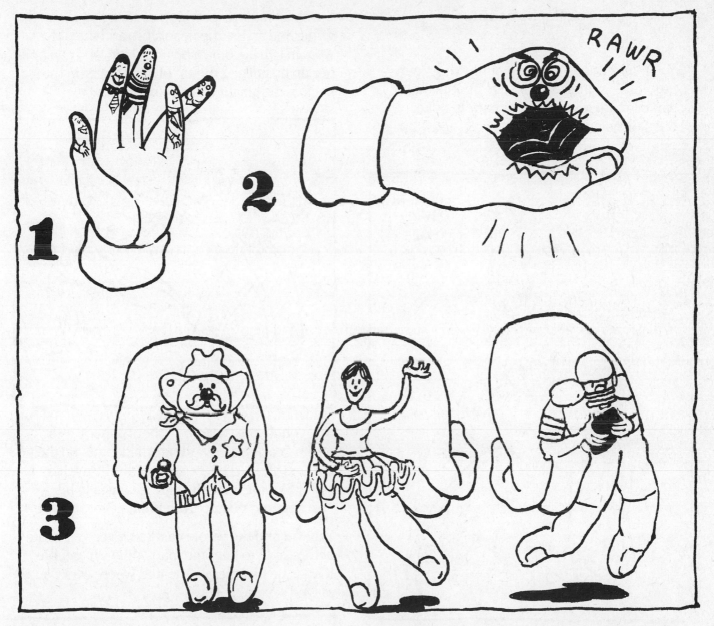

Here are a few more chances for your fingers to become stars of the silver screen.

1 If you have some fine-point, washable, felt-tipped pens, use them to draw some tiny faces on each of your fingertips. Now you have five or ten actors ready to perform!

2 If you like larger puppets, try the hand puppet shown in the second picture. Bunch your hand into a fist, add eyes and a nose and all the trimmings, and *presto!* Instant puppet with a big mouth! This one makes a good monster or giant, but is also capable of playing funny roles in comedy plays.

3 With the other hand, you could make a cowboy (or football player, or ballet dancer or...) hand puppet like the one in the picture. The fingers are the legs and the body is drawn on the back of the hand.

Hanky Puppets

The Hanky People

You might think twice about blowing your nose after seeing the strange people that can be made out of an ordinary handkerchief or tissue.

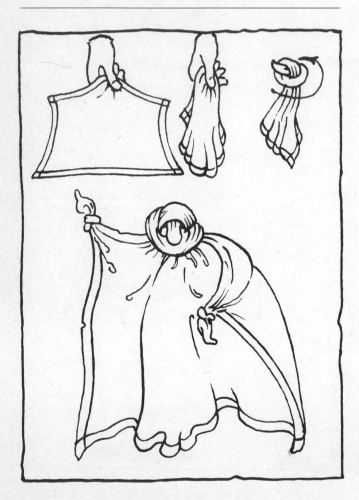

1 Tie a medium-sized knot in the center of one side of the hanky, then tie a small knot in each of the two corners on the same side, and you have a wizened old witch with a long flowing dress or a kindly old gypsy woman.

2 Slip a finger ring or loop of string on for a girdle and adjust the nose a bit, and the old woman can become a beautiful girl. You can hold her up by putting the tip of your finger in the back of the girdle, from below.

3 If you tie the bottom corners of her dress around each other, and tie small knots on the corners, the girl becomes that well-traveled sailor Sinbad, or, with slight changes in his costume and posture, the Villain.

You will find the whole cast to be very versatile actors, able to become many different people. It's a little like the old theater, where every actor played several parts.

Rabbit and Donkey

These two many-sided characters make good smart-aleck sidekicks for the other performers, but they can also take on a lead part with the greatest of ease. They are both masters of disguise, and by shortening their ears or adjusting their faces, they can look like anything from a horse, to a dog, a kangaroo to a giraffe.

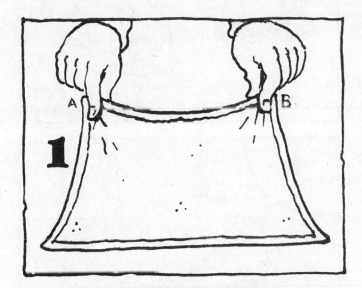

1 They are both formed with one simple knot. Fold the hanky in half, bringing the two top corners together (A and B).

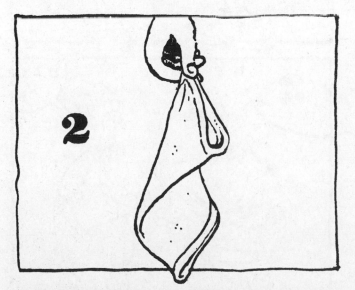

2 Hold the handkerchief in the right hand by the corners AB, and let the rest hang limp.

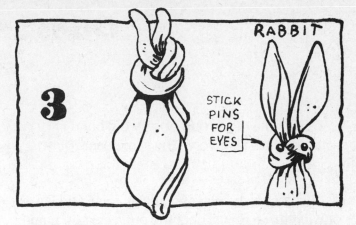

3 Tie a knot as shown just below the corners and change the ears, and you have a Rabbit.

4 By pulling on his nose and shortening his ears, you can turn Rabbit into Donkey. By shortening the ears even more, Donkey becomes Horse or whatever your imagination says. After all, that's who's in charge here!

5 All of these characters can be held from underneath by the hand or index finger. With Rabbit, your index finger can hold up the head, and your thumb and middle fingers can form the front paws, underneath the cloth.

Odds and Evens

PLAYERS:
2 OR 3

This is one of a group of very old hand games that all involve the same basic play.

1 All at once, the players quickly raise and lower one fist three times, opening out a certain number of fingers on the third 'throw.' This motion is done as if they were knocking on a table three times with their knuckles, then opening out their fingers on the third knock.

2 Players open out either one or two fingers on the third shake of the fist.

3 The first player calls out 'Odd!' or 'Even!' as the hands come down, but *just before the fingers open*. The object is to guess whether both players will open out the same number of fingers (even) or a different number (odd).

4 If you guess right, you score one point and get another turn at guessing. If you guess wrong, you lose your turn, and the other player calls odd or even on the next round.

5 If there are three players, you can play 'Odd Man Out.' Players stick out one or two fingers on the third shake as before, but this time no one calls odd or even. Instead, the player with a different number of fingers from the other two scores one point.

Scissors, Paper, Rock

PLAYERS:
2 OR 3

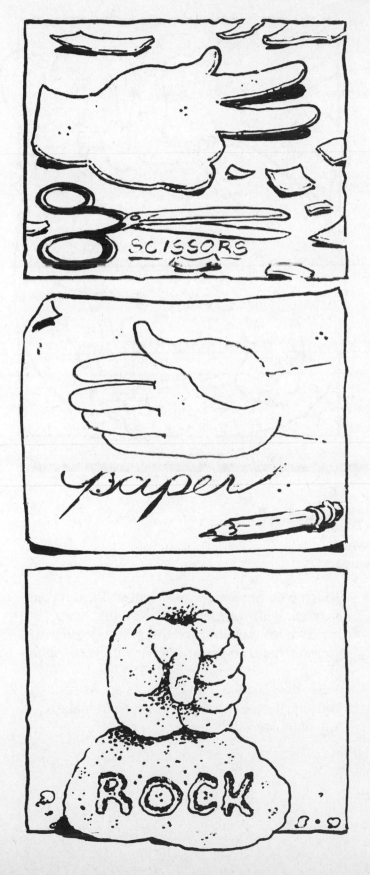

This hand game comes from ancient Rome, but it has also been known for centuries in Japan as the game of Janken. It has traveled all around the globe in the hands of young travelers, and people everywhere seem to know of it.

1 It is played in the same manner as the last two games: on the count of three, players hold out one hand and open a certain number of fingers.
2 Players can open out either all five fingers, two fingers or no fingers at all. Five fingers represent *paper,* two fingers represent *scissors* and no fingers (the fist) represent *rock.*
3 In a game of two players, if both players open out the same sign, it's a draw, and a point goes to the cat (whether it's an imaginary one or a real pet). If they open out different signs, this is how they score:

Scissors wins over *paper* because they can cut it.
Paper wins over *rock* because it can wrap it.
Rock wins over *scissors* because it can break them.

The winner of the round scores one point.
4 If there are three players, each scores according to what the other players have. For example, if each player has a different sign, no one wins because they cancel each other out. One point for the cat. If the other two players have paper and you have scissors, you win the round and score *two* points. If two players have rock, and you have scissors, they both win over you, but it is a draw between them, so they get only one point each instead of two.

Animal Crack-ups

PLAYERS:
2, 3 OR 4

Animal Crack-ups is a new version of Odds and Evens that is guaranteed to have you cracking up with laughter in no time flat.

1 Each player decides on an animal he wants to imitate (or you could draw names from a hat) and what the animal's call-of-the-wild sounds like. The call should be short and simple, like 'meow,' 'arf arf,' 'oink,' 'blub blub' or whatever. Pay close attention to everyone else's call.
2 All at once the players bring their hands down three times (see the last game), and the third time, they open out one, two or three fingers.
3 If two players have the same number of fingers out, they try to be the first to say the other's animal call. The first one to say the other's call wins the round and scores one point.

Right, Wrong!

PLAYERS:
ANY NUMBER

Touch your nose with your right hand, and your right ear with your left hand. Now clap your hands in front of you, and touch your nose with your *left* hand and your *left* ear with your *right* hand.

See how fast you can keep this up. As soon as you slip, it's the other player's turn to make a fool of himself!

Seven Old Counting-out Games

PLACERS:
2 OR MORE

These games are like the classic 'eeny meeny minie moe…,' and the more players you can get in on them the better. These rhymes can be used for deciding who is 'It' or who is the first player, or you can use them as games by themselves.

1 The players gather in a circle, and the person reciting the rhyme points at each player, one after the other, at the same time as he says each word of the poem. (Sometimes it is every two words, as in eeny meeny minie moe.)
2 The last person pointed at is out.
3 If the person reciting goes out, he still carries on the counting.
4 This goes on until only one player is left. This person is It.
5 You could also say that this player is the winner and scores one point.
6 In some games, the players hold out two hands, which must both be counted off before the player is out.
7 Sometimes the person saying the rhyme has to slap the finger of the person he points to last, as he says the last word. If he succeeds, the person hit has to become the reciter.

The combinations seem unlimited, and so do the number of rhymes and rhyming games, but try out these seven old favorites, then invent some new ones of your own.

Engine, Engine

Engine, engine, number nine,
Rollin' down Chicago line;
If that train should jump the track,
Do you want your money back?

The player pointed to on the word 'back' answers either yes or no, and the person counting out recites this next verse, pointing at players as before.

Y-e-s spells yes (or N-o spells no)
So out you must *go!*

The player pointed to on the word 'go' is out.

One Potato

1 Players put forward both fists. These are the potatoes.
2 If you are doing the counting out, tap each player's two potatoes, one at a time with one of your own potatoes, as you say each *number* in the rhyme. Count your own two fists as well.
3 On the last word of the rhyme ('more'), the potato touched must be taken away. This goes on until only one is left. Here is the rhyme:

One potato, two potatoes,
Three potatoes, four;
Five potatoes, six potatoes,
Seven potatoes, *more.*

Letter Out

This version of the counting-out game tends to go on for quite a while because there is less chance of getting caught.

1 The person counting recites the alphabet, pointing to one player after the other as he recites each letter.

2 If the person counting happens to be pointing at you when he says the first letter of your first name (J for John, etc.), then you are out.

These next four rhymes are counted out in the usual way; point at one player after another as you say each section of the rhyme. The lines are marked off so you can see how to do it, except for this first one, which counts out on each word.

My Mother

My mother and your mother live across the way,
One fifty-five North Broadway.
Every night they have a fight
And this is what they say:
Acka backa, soda cracka,
Acka backa boo.
If your daddy chews tobacco,
Out go Y.O.U.!!

Dickery Dickery

Dickery / dickery / dare, /
The pig / flew up / in the air; /
The man / in brown /
Soon brought / him down, /
Dickery / dickery / dare. /

Intry Mintry

Intry / mintry / peppery / corn, /
Apple / seed and / apple / thorn. /
Wire, / briar, / limber lock, /
Three / geese / to make / a flock. /
One / flew east / and one / flew west, /
One / flew over / the cuckoo's / nest. /

Ibbity Bibbity

Ibbity / bibbity / sibbity / Sam, /
Ibbity / bibbity / steamboat. /
Up the river, / down the river, /
Out / goes / *you!* /

Thumb Breaking, Nose Snapping

Yeow! Your friends will shudder with sympathy as they watch you tear your thumb off – and yet, you don't even seem to notice! As a matter of fact, when they look closely your thumb is still in one piece, unharmed and wiggling happily!

Frighten them some more by breaking your thumb again, and then, just to keep them on the edge, reach up and crack the bone in your nose. Snap! Crackle! Pop! Before they start looking for a phone to call an ambulance you'd better show them that you are, in fact, undamaged. You have merely performed a couple of simple, and impressive, finger tricks.

appears as if you're holding the left thumb between your right thumb and index finger.
4 Wiggle the 'thumb' for a second, then slowly move your right hand to the right. To the audience, who sees only the back of the left hand, it appears as if you are pulling your left thumb right off!

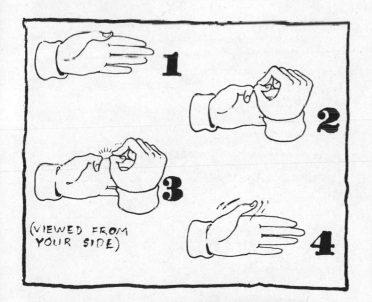

(VIEWED FROM YOUR SIDE)

1 For the first one, you need only two hands. Hold the left hand in front of you, as if you were reading your palm, with the fingers pointing to the right, and the palm toward you. Tell your friends that you are going to break off your thumb.
2 Your right hand then reaches over and appears to grab your left thumb.
3 In reality, as your right hand hides your left from view for a moment, you bend the left thumb down at the joint as shown in the picture. It

1 Before they get a chance to recover, spring the nose-cracking stunt on them. Hold your nose with both hands as shown in the picture, and face your friends.
2 In this position, your thumbs should be in front of your mouth and hidden by your hands.
3 Move your nose from side to side with your hands, and at the same time click your thumbnails against your teeth. To your friends it will look and sound as if you are tearing your nose right off!

MIND GAMES

Hard and Soft

Caution! We are now entering the mysterious realm of the mind! Heaven only knows how we found it in the first place – psychologists (the folks who study the mind) and thinkers down through the ages have disagreed on the position, use and meaning of the mind, and even whether it exists or not.

It hides out somewhere in our brain, sometimes letting us catch its workings, but more often than not keeping us totally in the dark.

The study of the mind is filled with questions, of which 'Why?' is perhaps the most burning. 'Why me?' is the next most burning. 'How high is the sky?' has also been heard echoing through the halls of learning, along with 'Is there really a Santa Claus?' I'll say one thing for these psychologists, they're a curious bunch . . . .

The only thing that all the experts seem able to agree on is that the mind can be a lot of fun when it puts its mind to it. Mind you, it can also be a downright nuisance: cranky, selfish, forgetful and...uh...I forget what else....

What the mind really needs, when it gets too lazy, is a spot of mental gymnastics to get the juices flowing.

If mental gymnastics sounds like your prescription, try out some of the hard- and soft-boiled mind games in this chapter. You will soon have the pesky critter jumping through mental hoops and eating out of your hand.

These games help to develop your powers of observation and deduction, sharpen your mental reflexes and generally improve your outlook on life. Try them! Your mind will thank you.

How Many Birds in the Bush?

PLAYERS:
2 OR MORE

You know what they say, 'A bird in the hand is worth two in the bush.' The problem with counting birds in bushes is that often you can't see the birds for the leaves, even though you know they're there because you can hear their chirping and chattering. Just try to count birds by listening to their songs and you'll see what I mean.

Try this: use coins instead of birds and your hands instead of a bush.

1 One player puts an unknown number of coins (more than three) in his cupped hands and shakes them.
2 'How many birds in the bush?' the player asks, and all the other players guess, one at a time.
3 The ones who guess correctly win one point. If only one person guesses right, he gets to shake the 'birds' for the next round.

In the Attic

PLAYERS:
2 OR MORE

All kinds of crazy things go on in the attic when the lights are out and people are asleep. You can find anything there, from an allomorph alliterating to a zygote zigzagging. What else can you think of that goes on in the attic?

1 Start the game off by saying something like, 'In the attic there's an acrobat admiring.'
2 The next player starts his sentence off in the same way, but the last two words must begin with B.
3 The third player ends his sentence with two words starting with C, and so on through the alphabet.
4 If you had your English teacher with you, he or she might tell you that the last two words in each sentence must be a noun and a participle, but who brings his English teacher home, anyway?
5 Here's a sample game among three players just starting:

1 In the attic there's an aardvark applauding.
2 In the attic there's a bird beaming.
3 In the attic there's a cat calling.
1 In the attic there's a dog digging.
2 In the attic there's an elf eating.
3 In the attic there's a philosopher frying.

Oops! Hold it! That last one doesn't count because 'philosopher' does *not* start with an F even though it starts with an F sound. Player three loses one point and player one starts off again at F.
6 You also lose a point if you can't think of anything to say right away, and break the rhythm of the game. Keep the game moving very quickly all the way to 'zebras zipping,' and then start back at A again.
7 If you want, you can leave out the last three letters, X, Y and Z, to make the game move even faster.

Eye Spy

PLAYERS:
2 OR MORE

I spy with my little eye something that is…
blue!

    This game must be the goldenest oldie
in the book, but if you don't already know it,
it's never too late to learn.

1 One player is chosen to start. If it's you, look
around and secretly choose an object or patch
of color. It could be anything from a thin pink
stripe on a scarf to the color of the rug, or someone's eyes.
2 Say the rhyme above ('I spy…') and let the
others know the color.
3 The other players can only make guesses
about which object they think you spy, and you
must answer their guesses with only 'yes' or 'no.'
4 The player who first guesses the correct object
wins that round and scores one point.
5 For the next round the winner becomes the
spy who chooses an object that everyone else
must guess….
6 A sample game might go like this:

You say aloud, 'I spy with my little eye something that is pink!' Don't give it away by looking
at what you spy. The other players then ask
questions like 'Is it Dad's nose?' 'Is it the cap on
the thermos?' 'Is it my lucky rabbit's foot?' until
someone guesses correctly. That player 'spies'
for the next round.

7 There is another way to play this game, and
that is to give the first letter of the object's name
as a clue instead of its color. In this case you say,
'I spy with my little eye something that starts
with…X?!'

Simon Says

PLAYERS:
2 OR MORE

This old game has many versions and variations, and is so popular that people are
named after it! When our great-grandparents
played it as children, they probably said,
'The Sultan says….' But the basic game has
remained unchanged for years and years.

1 One player is chosen to be Simon. This player
must perform actions, which the others copy.
2 With each action, Simon says, 'Simon says do
this!' or 'Simon says touch your head!' or
whatever.
3 If Simon says only 'Do this!' you must not do it.
4 If he says one thing and does another, you
must only do what Simon *says*.
5 For example, Simon might say, 'Simon says
touch your left elbow' and instead touch his
right elbow. If *you* touch your right elbow, you
are out of the game.
6 If you copy Simon's action when he says only
'Do this,' you are out of the game.
7 The last player left in the game scores one
point and becomes Simon for the next round.

Open It!

PLAYERS:
4 OR MORE

This is an old guessing game like 'Button, Button.'

1 The players divide into two teams and sit on opposite sides.
2 The players of one team go into a huddle and pass a coin or some other small object from one hand to another.
3 When they have secretly decided which hand the coin should remain in, they hold their closed fists in front of them and face their opponents, who have to guess which fist holds the coin.

4 If Team Two thinks a hand is empty, one of them gives the order 'Take it away,' and that hand is put behind its owner's back.
5 If Team Two thinks it knows which of the hands holds the coin, a player gives the order 'Open it' to the hand, which must then do so.
6 If Team Two orders an empty hand to open, or if it orders the coin-holding hand to be taken away, it loses that round, and Team One scores one point and gets another turn.
7 If Team Two finds the coin, they score one point, and it is their turn to hide the coin from the other team.

Geography

PLAYERS:
2 OR MORE

1 The first player says the name of a village, town, city, state, province, country, continent, river, lake or ocean that first springs into his or her mind.
2 The second player must then say the name of a village, town, city, etc., that begins with the same letter the first name *ended* with.
3 For instance, let's say that the first player says 'Saskatchewan.' The next player must then say the name of someplace geographic that starts with letter N.
4 The game might go like this: Nicaragua... Africa...Allansville...Europe...Egypt... Toronto...Oxford...and so on. Using a map will make the game go much faster.
5 If you can't think of anything that hasn't already been said, you are out of the game. The last person left wins the round and scores one point.

Backwords

PLAYERS:
ANY NUMBER

...ha ha ha bicycle a on riding cigar a smoking Pa seen you have

Hang on everyone! It's time to put your mind in reverse!

1 All the sentences shown below must be said backward after hearing them read once forward.
2 The first player reads one of the sentences aloud and then points at one of the other players.
3 That player must say the phrase from memory, but backward! For example, 'Cat's in the cupboard' would come out as 'Cupboard the in cat's.'
4 If the player who is doing the reverse reciting makes a slip, the first player points at another player.
5 The first person to get it right wins the round and scores one point. The winner reads a sentence aloud for the next round.
6 If no one gets it right, the first player reads another sentence.
7 It's best to start off with one of the first four shorter sentences until everyone's motor warms up a bit:

1 The flowers were brightly singing.
2 I'm a knock-kneed chicken.
3 I saw Esau sitting on the seesaw.
4 Everyone is in the best seat.
5 Have you seen Pa smoking a cigar, riding on a bicycle, ha ha ha.
6 The train I came in has not arrived.
7 Acka backa soda cracka, acka backa boo.
8 Some men are wise and some are otherwise.
9 Mary had a little lamb, a little toast, a little jam.
10 Things are more like they are now than they ever were before.
11 I can't figure out where I leave off and everyone else begins.
12 Would you rather be a bigger fool than you look, or look a bigger fool than you are?

8 Invent some variations for this game with your own zany sentences and one-liners!

Verse-atility

PLAYERS:
ANY NUMBER

This game is just the thing to sweep the cobwebs out of the corners of your cerebrum (a part of your brain, silly!).

1 Each player picks a different one of the verses below and memorizes it.

Jack and Jill
Went up the hill
To fetch a pail
Of water.

I eat my peas with honey,
I've done it all my life.
It makes the peas taste funny,
But it keeps them on the knife.

Nothing to do but work!
Nothing! Alas! Alack!
Nowhere to go but out!
Nowhere to come but back!

As I was sitting in my chair,
I *knew* the bottom wasn't there.
Nor legs nor back, but *I just sat,*
Ignoring little things like that.

Humpty Dumpty
Sat on the wall,
Humpty Dumpty
Had a great fall.

As I was going up the stair,
I met a man who wasn't there.
He wasn't there again today!
I wish that man would go away!

I put my hat upon my head
And walked into the strand,
And there I met another man
Whose hat was in his hand.

I've never had a piece of toast
Particularly long and wide,
But fell upon the sanded floor
And always on the buttered side.

Some of the verses are harder to memorize than others, so younger players should choose an easy one. Once everyone has memorized a verse, take turns trying the following antics.

2 In your head, count the number of words in your verse. Have someone else check it with the one in the book.

3 Now say your verse out loud, numbering each word. If your verse is Jack and Jill, start like this: 1 Jack, 2 and, 3 Jill, 4 went, 5 up....

4 Now say your poem backward. (Water of pail a fetch to....)

5 Now try saying your verse out loud, clapping on each *second* word and snapping your fingers on each *third* word. For example, 'Jack and(clap) Jill(snap) went up(clap) the(snap) hill....'

6 By now, everyone's mind should be going soft around the edges. To finish the job, have all players recite their verses at once.

7 For each of the above antics that you did right, give yourself one point. Everyone is bound to make plenty of mistakes on the first round, so give it a couple more tries with the same verse, then try another one.

Memory

PLASERS:
2 OR MORE

This game will test your powers of memory like Kim's Game, but it's much simpler and faster moving, and especially fun with a large group of people.

1 Make a list of ten simple words, numbering them from one to ten.
2 Read the list, including numbers, out loud to the group.
3 Now say any number from one to ten.
4 The first player to tell you what word on the list has that number, scores one point.
5 After a few rounds of this, you might want to try something different. Make a new list and read it out loud, but this time, read it in any order except the right order. The first player who can say the list in the proper order scores a big five (count 'em!) points and wins the game!

Conversation

PLAYERS:
3 OR MORE

Anyone who listened in on the conversation between the players of this game would think that the people talking were pretty strange, because the words just don't seem to make sense! For one thing, none of the sentences are more than two words long, and for another thing, it sounds more like some kind of weird poem than an actual conversation.

1 The first player starts by saying a two-word sentence made up of one noun and one verb, in that order (e.g. Rain falls).

2 The second player also says a two-word sentence, but the first word (the noun) must start with the *same two letters* as the second word (the verb) of the last player's sentence.
3 A sample 'conversation' might go like this:

Time flies.
Fleas jump.
Jugglers toss.
Toast burns.
Birds fly.

Oops! That last sentence just won't do! That player is out! Can you see why? The last player left in the game scores two points and wins the round.

Jotto

PLAYERS:
2

1 The object of the game is to guess the five-letter word that the other player is thinking of, while that player is at the same time trying to guess your own secret word. If you like, you can use a paper and pencil to help you figure out the word.
2 Each player thinks of or writes down a five-letter word whose letters are all different.
3 Players take turns guessing which five-letter word they think the other player has written down.
4 You can answer each other's guesses only by saying *how many letters* in the word guessed are also in your secret word. Don't say which letters they are, just how many. For instance, if your word is 'words', and the other player guesses 'guest', you tell him that one letter in 'guest' is also in your word.
5 On a piece of paper write down all the words you guess, with the number of letters right. At the bottom of the sheet write out the alphabet. If you guess a word that has *no* letters common to the other player's word, cross out the letters that are in the word you guessed from the alphabet....These clues will help you in your word detective work.
6 By looking carefully at the words you've guessed, you should be able to take out the letters that are not in the other player's secret word. For example, let's say you guess 'jerks', and the other player tells you that there is one letter in 'jerks' that is also in his secret word. Then you guess 'jerky' and the other player tells you that there are no letters in 'jerky' that are in his secret word. Well, you can figure out that the J, E, R, and K in jerks are not in the secret word because they are also in 'jerky', which has no letters in the secret word. Therefore, the letter in 'jerks' that is in the other player's secret word must be the S.
7 The first player to guess the other player's word is the winner!

Alphabetical

PLAYERS:
ANY NUMBER

1 The first player starts out by saying 'I have an _____.' The blank must be filled with a word that starts with the letter A.
2 The second player repeats the first player's sentence, adding on a phrase that contains a noun starting with the letter B.
3 The third player repeats the second player's sentence and adds on a phrase containing a noun or verb that begins with C.
4 For example, a game with three players might start like this:

1 I have an *aardvark*.
2 I have an aardvark with a *balloon*.
3 I have an aardvark with a balloon in a *can*.
1 I have an aardvark with a balloon in a can for my *Dad*.
2 I have an aardvark with a balloon in a can for my Dad to *eat*.

5 The game goes on like this until you have gone right through the alphabet. If you want to make things a little simpler, leave off the last three letters of the alphabet, X, Y and Z.
6 This is the kind of game where a dictionary might help. Also a very good memory would help, as it becomes harder and harder to remember the whole sentence. If you make a mistake, you are out of the game. The last player left wins that round and scores one point.

Twenty Questions

PLACES:
2 OR MORE

1 The object of this game is to guess the secret object chosen by the first player by asking 20 questions that the first player must answer with only 'yes' or 'no.'

2 The first player thinks of an object or thing, and tells the other players whether the thing he is thinking of is animal, mineral or vegetable. It must be something that fits one of the three categories, but it can't fit in more than one category. For example, you can't think of anything like a house, which is made up of vegetable (wood) and mineral (metal) substances.

3 After the first player has chosen a word, the other players then take turns asking questions that can be answered by 'yes' or 'no.' At first, it's best to ask very general questions and narrow it down later.

4 The first player keeps track of the number of questions asked, and if no one has guessed what the secret object is by the twentieth question, the first player wins the game and scores one point, and then he or she thinks of another object for the next round.

5 The player who guesses the object wins one point and takes the place of the first player.

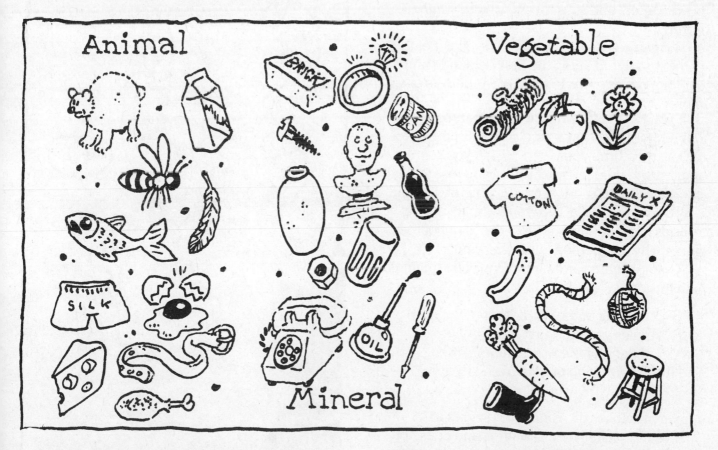

This list shows some of the things in each group and should help you decide:

Animal – animals, bugs, fish, etc., or anything made from them: leather, wool, silk, eggs, milk, cheese, feathers, fur, etc.

Mineral – metal, stone, plastic, glass, ceramics, oil products or anything synthetic.

Vegetable – plants or anything made from them: wood, cotton, paper, rubber, rope, string, etc.

Ghosts

PLAYERS:
2 TO 5

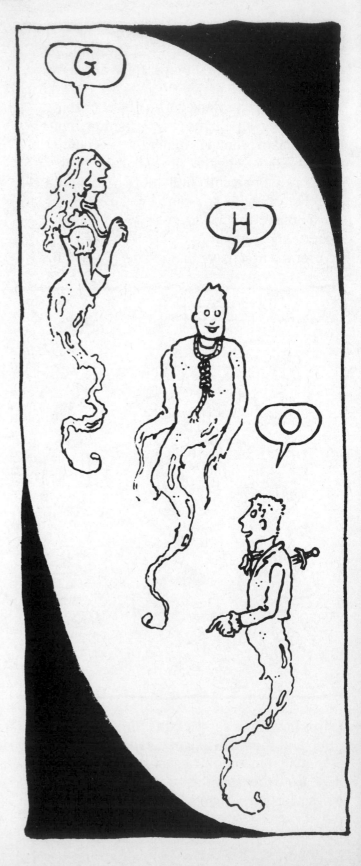

Who's afraid of ghosts? Not me! Especially since the 'Ghosts' I'm talking about is the name of this great game.

1 The first player thinks of any word, then says the first letter of that word out loud.
2 The second player must then think of a word beginning with that letter and say this word's *second* letter out loud.
3 The next player then thinks of any word starting with the first two letters that have already been named, and says this new word's *third* letter.
4 The game goes on like this. The object of the game is to avoid being the first person to finish spelling out any whole word of five letters or more.
5 If you finish any word of five letters long or longer, you lose that round and score the letter G. The next time you lose a round, you score the letter H, and the next round you lose you score an O, then an S, then a T, which, when put together spell GHOST. Anyone who loses five rounds and becomes a Ghost drops out of the game. The last person left is the winner!
6 A sample game among three players might go like this:

1 'G' (Thinking of the word *ghost*)
2 'I' (Thinking of the word *give*)
3 'A' (Thinking of the word *giant*)
1 'N' (Also thinking of *giant*)
2 'T' (Finishes the word)

Player two loses the round and scores a G.
7 If you think a player is bluffing and does not have a real word in mind when saying his letter, you may challenge him. If he can't tell you what word he has in mind, he loses the round. If he really *does* have a word in mind and you challenge him, you lose the round.

Head to Feet

PLAYERS:
ANY NUMBER

This is another mind game that requires pencil and paper.

1 The only other things you'll need are two short words, both with the same number of letters. Everyone writes down the two agreed-upon words on his sheet of paper.

2 The object of the game is to magically change the first word into the second word, one step at a time.

3 With each step, you can only change one letter, and each new step must also be a real word.

4 Whoever changes the first word into the second word in the fewest steps is the winner. In the event of a tie, both players win.

5 For example, this is how to change the word *head* into *feet* in the fewest possible steps:

head
heed
feed
feet

In each step, only one letter has been changed, and each is a real word.

6 Other combinations you might try are: *dog* to *cat*, *boy* to *man*, *word* to *rock*, *flour* to *bread*, and *wind* to *calm*.

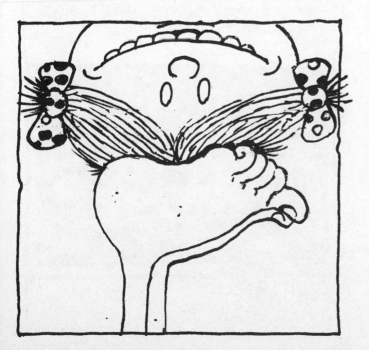

Boutes-rimes

PLAYERS:
2 OR MORE

One version of this game goes all the way back to the year 1648, when it was invented in France by the poet Dulos. It became fashionable as a parlor game among the folks rich enough to have parlors, and it spread like hot butter to parlors all over Europe.

Having been invented by a poet, it is, naturally enough, a very poetic game.

1 The first player says four words out loud. The first and third words must rhyme with each other, and the second and fourth words must rhyme with each other. For example, the four words might be 'try,' 'can,' 'pry' and 'pan.'

2 The other players will each need a pencil and paper. They try to write a four-line poem using each of the four words as the last word of a line. The words have to be used in the order they were written.

3 The first person to finish the poem is the winner, but only if the poem makes some kind of sense. If it doesn't, then the second player to finish is the winner – if *his* poem makes sense. Let everyone finish his poem, and then read them all out loud.

4 Here is an example, using the four words above:

Oh, everything did I try
To get my lunch from its can.
For I've nothing with which to pry,
Just a rusty old dust pan....

Well, it's a bit rough around the edges, but it fills the bill.

COUNT ME IN!

Fun With Numbers

Like almost everything else, the discovery of numbers is blamed on our lovable ancestor, the caveperson, who found them very handy for keeping track of how many fingers and toes were on each hand and foot.

The ancient Egyptians, Babylonians, Greeks and Romans all had their own number systems, but most were clumsy and difficult to use, so they gradually died out. One of the more sensible systems did manage to survive, though – Arabic numerals, which are the numbers that most of the world uses today.

Numbers soon had a science all their own, called 'mathematics.' Mathematicians soon realized that there were many different and stranger kinds of numbers than the ones you use to count apples and oranges.

Start with two ordinary hands, and you've got your <u>digits</u> from zero to nine. Combine them in every possible way and you get the <u>counting numbers</u> up to infinity. Take them all away and you have the <u>negative numbers</u> down to infinity. Throw these in with the counting numbers, and you have the <u>integers</u>.

Look in between each integer and you'll see an infinity of <u>fractions</u>. Add these to the integers and you have what are called the <u>rational numbers</u>. These, together with the notorious <u>irrational numbers</u>, form what we know as the <u>real number system</u>, with which we can add, subtract, multiply, divide, count, describe and measure.

fractions + integers = rational numbers

Now we are into the weird realm of number theory. Mutter a few magic axioms, and you get the <u>prime numbers</u>, <u>composite numbers</u>, <u>complex numbers</u> and a lot of other strange things. Wave an equation or two over the whole batch and in a twinkling of an eye, <u>transinfinite numbers</u> appear, along with their funny little friends, the <u>infinite</u> and <u>infinitesimal numbers</u>.

Next thing you know, you've got more square roots, geometry, algebra, congruences, set theories and reciprocals than you can shake a fistful of digits at.

Aside from playing a large part in almost everything, from the pyramids and space flight to money and time, numbers can also be a lot of fun, as this chapter sets out to prove. And don't you let any math teacher tell you otherwise!

Hul Gul

PLAYERS:
2 OR MORE

This game has been popular ever since children played it in ancient Greece. It is also a great game for practicing math skills.

1 Each player needs the same number of counters. You can use anything small, such as coins, bits of paper, pebbles or whatever you can find. Ten counters each is a good number to start with.

2 Hide a few counters in your fist.

3 Turn to another player and say 'Hul Gul.'

4 The other player replies 'Handful!'

5 Then you say 'How many?'

6 Each player then tries to guess how many counters you have in your fist. No two players can guess the same number.

7 If a player guesses right, that player gets to keep all the counters that are in your hand.

8 If other players guess too high, they each must give you some of their counters to make up the difference between their guess and the real number of counters. For example, if you have five counters in your hand, and another player guesses twelve, he must give you seven counters.

9 If the other players guess too low, they each must give you five counters. Or they must give you the smaller half of their counters if they have less than ten (four if each has only nine or eight, three for seven or six, and so on).

10 Next turn, the player who guessed right gets to hide some counters in his or her hand. If no one guessed right, it's your turn again.

11 The game is over when one player has won all the counters.

Nim

PLAYERS:
2 OR **3**

This is one member of a large family of take-away games that involve plenty of rapid number-thinking. These games are usually very simple to play, and yet they can be very challenging, especially if you play with three players instead of the usual two.

1 Start with any number of matches, toothpicks or coins and lay them down in any number of rows, with any number of objects per row.

2 Players take turns picking up objects. You can pick up as many as you like, as long as they are *side-by-side in the same row*. For example, if another player picks up the middle object from a row of seven, you can't pick up the other six objects left at once because there is a gap between the two groups of three.

3 The person who picks up the last object is the loser.

4 A good pattern to start the game with is four rows of objects with one in the first row, three in the second, five in the third and seven in the fourth row.

Odd Wins

PLAYERS:
2

1 All you need to play is an odd number of toothpicks, coins, pebbles or whatever. You should have at least 15 altogether, the more the merrier.
2 Throw the counters in a heap on the table or floor.
3 Players take turns taking counters from the pile. They can take one, two or three counters at a time.
4 This goes on until there are no counters left in the pile.
5 Count up each player's counters. The winner is the player who ends up with an odd number of counters.

Up to a Hundred

PLAYERS:
2 OR MORE

This is an adding-up game, and is great fun for the mathematically inclined. You can play it by doing the sums on paper or, if you're feeling really smart today, you can work them out in your head.

1 The first player writes down any number from one to nine.
2 The next player adds any other number from one to nine and writes the sum underneath the first number.
3 The players continue like this, each person adding any number from one to nine. The object of the game is to be the person whose final addition brings the sum to *exactly* 100.
4 This is harder than it sounds. You are trying to be the first person to bring it up to 100, and you are also trying to keep all the other players from finishing before you do.
5 Once you've tried this game, try playing it in reverse – subtract one-digit numbers from 100, and the first player to reach zero is the winner. Or, once you've exercised your brain cells a bit, you could try with numbers between one and 20 to reach a final sum of 517 or 739 or whatever. Try doing *those* sums in your head!

Abraca-algebra

Here is some helpful magic that you can perform with ordinary, everyday numbers. All you need is an understanding of basic arithmetic and a willing audience.

Age Calculator

This one is easy. Tell a friend that you are going to guess his or her age.

1 Ask this friend to multiply his age by three, without letting you know the answer.

2 Have your friend add six to the result, then divide the sum by three.

3 Now ask for the final answer.

4 Secretly subtract two from that number in your head, and the result is the person's age!

Dates, Events and Ages

1 Ask your friend to write down the following things, keeping them hidden from you:

1 The year of his birth.
2 The year that any memorable event happened in his life.
3 The number of people in the room.
4 How old he will be on December 31 of this year.
5 The number of years ago that the memorable event took place.

2 Now ask your friend to add up all the numbers.

3 Secretly (in your head or on paper) work out this math problem: multiply the present year by two, and to that answer add the number of people in the room. The answer will be the same as your friend's!

4 If you like math, read this to find out how it works: The year of your birth plus your age as of December 31 of this year always equals the present year. The same goes for the year that an event happened, plus how many years ago it was. For example, if you were born on June 23, 1972 you will be 13 on December 31, 1985 (which, for the sake of argument, we will say is the present year). Add 13 to 1972 and you get 1985, the 'present' year. If an important event happened in 1979 and you add 6 to that – which is the same number of years ago as 1979 – you get 1985 again.

You know that your friend's total is going to be twice the present year, plus the number of people in the room.

For a really spectacular effect, you could write the answer on a slip of paper beforehand, hand it to your friend to hold, and then have him work out the calculation the long way round. After he is done, let him open out the paper to see that you have already beaten him to the answer, before he even started!

Finger Computer

In school you might be learning one of these new finger-arithmetic systems that are taking the world of mathematics by storm. Ever since cavepeople started giving number-names to fingers and toes, humans have been using them to do more complicated math. Well, fingers anyway. The invention of shoes has made toes useless as calculators.

The finger computer described here is a very ancient system. It was used in Europe during the Middle Ages, but probably goes back a lot further than that. People in those days usually knew the multiplication tables up to 5 x 5, and found that this system came in very 'handy' for figuring out more complicated calculations.

For multiplying numbers between 6 and 10, use this method:

1 Starting with the little fingers, the fingers on each hand are given the values 6 through 10, as shown in the first picture.

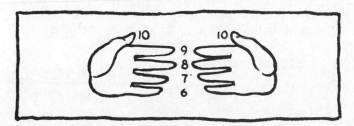

2 To multiply, for example, 6 x 8, touch the '6' finger on one hand (it doesn't matter which one you use) to the '8' finger on the other hand.

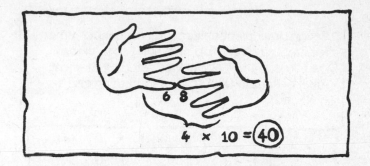

3 Count the lower fingers, *including the two touching fingers,* and multiply the total by 10.

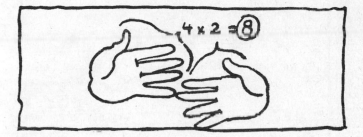

4 Multiply the number of upper fingers on the left hand by the number of upper fingers on the right hand.

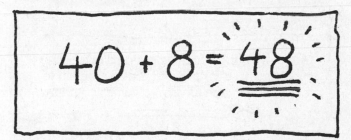

5 Add the two results, 40 and 8, together to get your final answer, 48.

6 Always remember that any number times zero equals zero, so if there are no upper numbers on one hand (as when multiplying any number by 10), you add zero, or nothing, to the number of lower fingers times 10.

There is a complicated way to use this finger computer to multiply numbers higher than 10, but if you can multiply the digits by themselves and by 10, you can usually break down larger calculations into smaller bits and figure them out, or do the calculation on paper.

BORED GAMES

Board Stiff? Try These!

People in ancient times didn't have much time for fun; they were too busy surviving. All they had time to think about was catching the next meal or keeping from being something else's next meal.

So, thousands of years ago, cavepeople weren't playing board games for laughs, but as a kind of magic ritual to bring about good hunting, or to keep hungry beasts away from the herds.

Later, when they became civilized and had more time to think about it, people began to realize how much fun board games could be!

The games in this chapter are very ancient (the oldest is 3000 years old), and come from Egypt, Rome, the Far East and every corner of the globe. Most modern board games are descendants of these ones.

Before you start reading the rules for the games, there are a few things you should know.

1 The playing pieces are known as <u>counters.</u>
2 In many games, the players start their counters on the side of the board nearest them, which is known as <u>home.</u>

3 In Checkers, you jump over a counter to take it off the board. In Chess, you land on the same square. There are other ways to take or trap counters, and the following standard names are used to describe them:

Short Jump This is the one used in Checkers, where you jump from the square or point right next to the opponent's counter, to the empty square or point right next to it on the other side.

Multiple Short Jump If, when you 'short jump' an opponent's counter, there is another one right next to your counter again, you may jump this one as well, as long as the square on the other side of it is empty. This is called the 'multiple short jump.'

Trap In some games, when you have two counters, one on each side of an opponent's counter, and in line with it, you have 'trapped' it and can remove it from the board.

Draw up your own boards on a sheet of paper.
Counters can be made from almost anything. Coins make good 'men,' but they are too easy to spend. You could also try matches, beans, macaroni, squares of paper or anything that can be painted or marked in different colors for different players. You can also leave your markers very plain or personalize them with decorations, designs or pictures.
The player with the lightest color counters always starts first.

Vice Versa

PLAYERS:
1 OR 2

1 As you can see from the picture, this game (actually it's more of a puzzle) is played on a strip of seven squares.
2 Three markers of one color are placed on one end, and three markers of another color on the other end (you could use three pennies and three dimes). The middle square is left empty.
3 The object of the game is to switch the two groups of counters, so that they are at opposite

ends, in as few moves as possible.
4 First a counter of one color is moved, then a counter of the other color. They can be moved one square forward, or jumped over another counter onto an empty square, but *they cannot move backward.*
5 If two people are playing, they play on separate boards, and the winner is the person who switches the counters in the fewest moves.

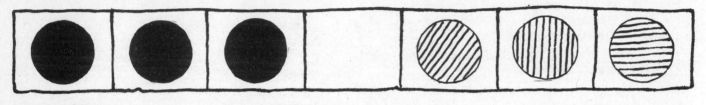

Latrunculi

PLAYERS:
2

Latrunculi (Latin for bandits or robbers) is an early form of Checkers that goes back to the days of Ancient Rome!

1 The playing board, as shown in the picture, is only four squares wide by four long, but every square can be played on.
2 Each player has four counters, which start on the back row, as shown.
3 As in Checkers, players take turns moving the counters forward (but not backward) diagonally, one square at a time. They can't move straight up or across, but must move on an angle.
4 Captures are made with the short jump or multiple short jump forward (see chapter introduction). As in Checkers, counters *can't jump backward!*
5 When a player's counter reaches the far side of the board, it is crowned a King (the other player places one of the captured counters of the same

color on top). The King can move and jump forward *and* backward, but still only diagonally.
6 The winner is the player who blocks or captures all the other player's counters, so that player can no longer move.

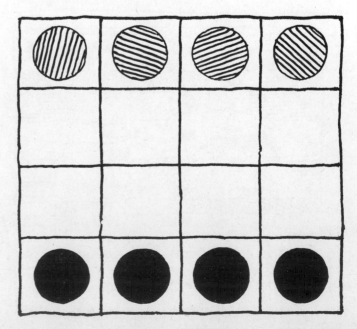

Five in a Row

PLAYERS:
2

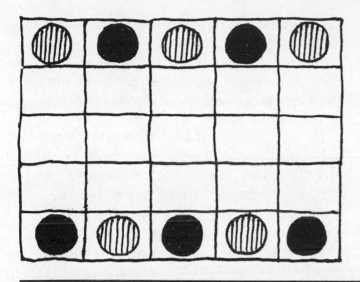

1 The playing board is five squares wide by five long.
2 Instead of starting at different ends of the board, the two players put their counters one after the other at both ends as shown.
3 Players take turns moving their own counters one square at a time. They can move forward, backward, across or diagonally, but they cannot jump.
4 The object of the game is to get all five of your own counters in a straight row, either up and down, across or diagonally. The first player to get a row of five wins!

Kono

PLAYERS:
2

Kono is a game that comes originally from Korea. In this version, no pieces are captured or taken off the board, but the game is still as exciting as a good comic book, or a game of Kick-the-Can.

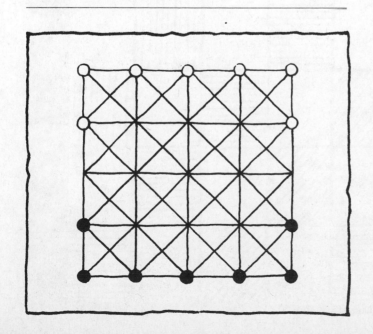

1 Kono is played on the crisscross board shown in the picture, on the points where the lines cross. Counters move along the lines.
2 Each of the two players has seven counters, which start out on the board in the arrangement shown.
3 Players take turns moving one counter at a time in any direction, one point at a time. Counters can move up or down, across or diagonally.
4 Counters can jump over any other counters, including their teammates, by the short jump or the multiple short jump (see chapter introduction), but no counters are captured or removed from the board.
5 The first player to get all seven counters arranged in the starting position at the opposite side of the board is the winner.

Bushwhackers!

PLAYERS:
2

Being a trapper in the days of the pioneers was not an easy job. Besides all the dangers from wild critters, there was always the chance of running into unfriendly Indians, who were protecting their hunting grounds from the paleface strangers. Sometimes Indian braves would lie in ambush, and bushwhack unsuspecting trappers. This game is played in much the same way.

1 Each player has one counter. One is the brave, and the other is the trapper.
2 Each player has his own playing board like the one in the picture. The brave is allowed to look at the trapper's board, but the trapper must *not* look at the brave's playing board. Other than this, the boards are the same.
3 The brave starts on any one of the three black squares at the top of his own board, and

the trapper starts on one of the black squares at the bottom of the other board.
4 Counters move only on the black squares. They move diagonally, in both directions, and can jump *sideways* (but *not* forward or back!) across a white square.
5 The trapper moves first. His object is to get to one of the three black squares at the other end of the board without landing on a square that the brave is already on, on the other board.
6 The brave tries to lie in wait for the trapper, on any square. He can move around or stay put on his turn, but may not 'attack' the trapper by moving onto a square that the trapper is already on.
7 If the trapper lands on a square that the brave is already on, on the other board, then the trapper is 'bushwhacked,' and the brave wins the game. But if the trapper makes it safely to the other end of the board without bumping into the sneaky brave, the trapper wins!

Senat

PLAYERS:
2

Anthropologists, the people who study people, had to do a little detective work to put together the rules of this game. It is one of the most ancient games around – over *3000* years old! These anthropologists looked at some old Egyptian paintings of people playing Senat, and by comparing it with games played today, they were able to figure out the original old Egyptian rules! And guess what else these dusty old professors found out about the game of Senat? It's fun!

1 The playing board is five squares wide by five long, and all squares can be played on. Each player needs twelve counters.

2 Players take turns putting *two* counters down at a time on any squares on the board except the center one, until all counters are on the board.

3 The player who put down the final two counters starts. If this player can't move, he can move one of the other player's counters out of the way, so he can move.

4 Players take turns moving one counter at a time, one square up, down or across, but *not* diagonally.

5 Counters are captured by *trapping* (see the introduction to this chapter for a description of trapping), but captures made before all the counters are on the board don't count. Captured counters are removed from the board.

6 If a player moves a counter between two of the other player's counters on purpose, it can't be trapped.

7 The object of the game is to capture or block all of the other player's counters.

8 Later in the game, if neither side can move, players count the number of counters left on the board. The player with the most counters left wins.

Block and Jump

PLAYERS:
2

This is one of the many variations of Senat that have been handed down over the years. It is also similar to Checkers, and it goes to show how easy it is to invent games by taking rules from other games and mixing them together.

1 It is played on a Senat board, five squares wide by five long, with all squares in use.
2 Each player uses twelve counters, as in Senat, but all are placed on the board at the beginning of the game, as shown in the picture.

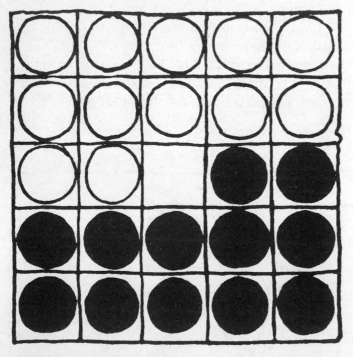

3 Players take turns moving one counter at a time, one square up, down or across, but not diagonally.
4 Captures are made by the short jump or the multiple short jump (see chapter introduction). Unlike Checkers, captures don't *have* to be made. That is, if you miss a chance to capture, or decide not to, your opponent *cannot* remove your counter from the board, like he can in Checkers.
5 The object of the game is to block or capture all of the other player's counters.

Alquerque

PLAYERS:
2

The Egyptians played this game over 2000 years ago. From there it moved into Arabia, then into Spain. The Spaniards took it to the New World with them and taught it to the natives of Central America, who still play it to this day.

1 The board has five points to a side. The counters play on the points (the places where the lines cross).
2 Each player has twelve counters, arranged as shown in the picture.

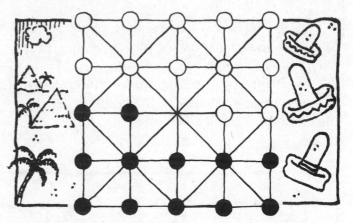

3 Players take turns moving onto any empty point. The counters move along the lines, forward, across and diagonally, but they can't move backward.
4 Players must capture, by the short jump or multiple short jump (see chapter introduction). The counters can jump in any direction except backward.
5 If one of your counters reaches the other player's side of the board, it must stay there until it can jump one of the other player's counters. Once it has done this it is crowned a King, (see Latrunculi) and it can move around again in any direction.
6 The winner is the player who captures or blocks all the other player's counters so they can't move. If neither player can move, the game is a draw or tie.

Three-man Morris

PLAYERS:
2

You don't need three people to play Three-man Morris. That's only the number of counters! Morris boards have been found scratched into the floors of ancient Egyptian temples and in the streets of Greek and Roman cities. They have been carved in the decks of Viking ships and in the tops of school desks. If you are traveling in Europe or Asia, kids will know this game everywhere you go. Why, even William Shakespeare played Morris! So, I'd like to take this opportunity to introduce you to a really great game, your friend and mine, Morris!

1 Three-man Morris is played on the funny-looking board shown in the picture.
2 Each of the two players has three counters.
3 Players take turns putting counters, one at a time, on any three points (where the lines cross) on the board.
4 Players can't move until all counters are on the board. Then they take turns moving one counter at a time along the lines, one point at a time (no fair jumping over a point), to any empty point.
5 The object of the game is to get three of your own counters in a row on any straight line on the board (horizontally, vertically or diagonally), while at the same time trying to keep the other player from doing the same thing.
6 How you place the counters at the very beginning of the game is important – pay close attention to what the other player is doing, and try to block as much as possible, as in Tic Tac Toe.

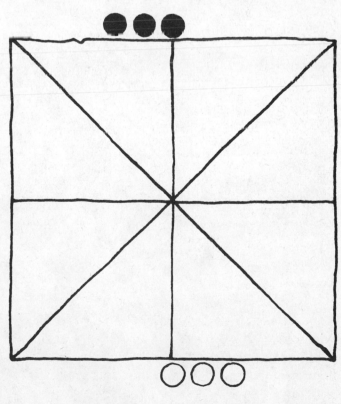

SCRAP HAPPY

Creative Recycling

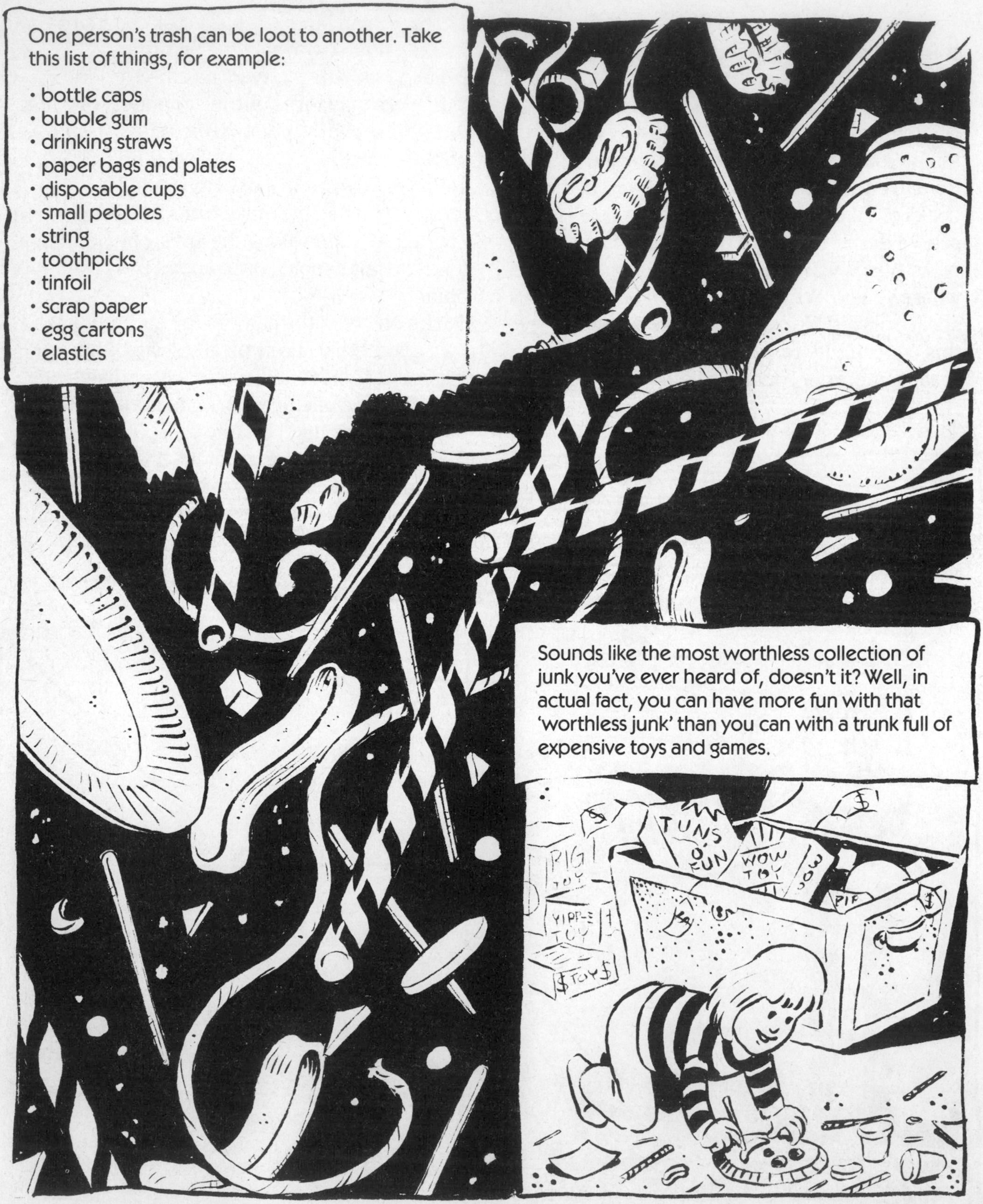

One person's trash can be loot to another. Take this list of things, for example:

- bottle caps
- bubble gum
- drinking straws
- paper bags and plates
- disposable cups
- small pebbles
- string
- toothpicks
- tinfoil
- scrap paper
- egg cartons
- elastics

Sounds like the most worthless collection of junk you've ever heard of, doesn't it? Well, in actual fact, you can have more fun with that 'worthless junk' than you can with a trunk full of expensive toys and games.

What's more, 'scrap' like this is easily found, doesn't cost a cent, and people will likely thank you for taking it away!

This chapter is full of suggestions for playing games by making all kinds of neat things with scrap, but it doesn't stop there. The only limit is your imagination, so see what kind of crazy and useful inventions you can make from trash.

Besides the raw materials, you will need things like scissors, glue, tape, markers, crayons and paint. Put them all together and you have a recipe for fun!

Disguises

Have you ever wanted to be a Frankenstein monster, an Indian brave, a pirate, a space cowboy, a robot, a witch or some other character from comics, stories or your own wild imagination?

With a few paper bags and plates, some pens or markers, glue, odds and ends and a little creativity, you can design and make some wacky masks and disguise yourself as the creature of your choice!

1 First, collect together all the things you think you may need. This list will help:

Tools
- scissors
- glue
- tape
- paint, markers, crayons or pens

Materials
- paper bags – all sizes
- string
- paper plates
- straws
- tinfoil
- egg cartons

2 Now let your imagination take over! There are hundreds of ways you can use your paper bags – smaller ones make good hats, and larger ones can be worn covering your whole head. You can even tear off the bottom of the bag to produce a 'convertible' mask.

3 Paper plates can be used as either hats or faces, or torn in half to make weird glasses, goggles or eye masks. Poke holes in the edge of the plate with a pencil point, and tie a string 'harness' to the plate to hold it on your head. Paper plates may be worn alone or with your bag masks.

4 Make sure that the bags and/or plates are clean. Always cut out a large nose or mouth hole for breathing.

5 Once you have figured out the basic shape of your mask, paint, draw or color the details on. Use glue or tape to stick on things like colored paper, tinfoil, straws, etc.

Bubbles

To make lots of bubbles you need only a little bit of soap solution, and if you take proper precautions and are very careful, you shouldn't even have to worry about spilling any.

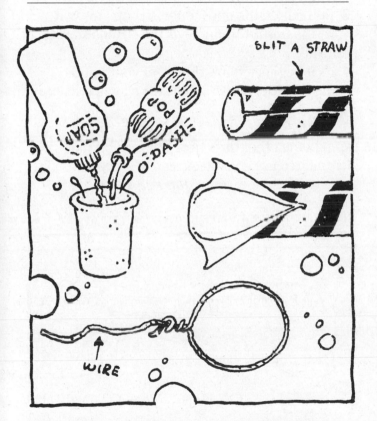

1 To make a great bubble solution, mix some liquid detergent with the same amount of water in a cup, and add a dash of soda pop or sugar. Mix well.

2 Now you need a bubble blower. You can make a simple one from a drinking straw. Cut a small slit in one side of one end, and fold back the paper along the slit. Dip this end in the bubble brew, and blow through the other end.

3 If you want to make bigger bubbles, you'll need some kind of hoop with a handle. A finger ring with a string tied to it works great, or you could bend a ring out of a paper clip, like the one in the picture.

Rip-off

PLAYERS:
ANY NUMBER

The more players you can round up for this game, the better.

1 Choose one player (draw straws, count out or whatever) to be the Banker.

2 The rest of the players each get a number. For instance, the first player is called Number One, the second player is called Number Two, and so on.

3 Each player is given three toothpicks, matches, coins or whatever. To make it more realistic, each player could draw three phony hundred-dollar bills.

4 The object of the game is for each player to try to hang onto his or her 'loot,' and for the Banker to try to collect all the loot, in order to go out.

5 The Banker takes the loot away like this: if he calls out your number and snaps his fingers before you do, you must give him one toothpick (or whatever you're using as loot).

6 If a player snaps his fingers by mistake, he or she loses one toothpick. For example, if the Banker says 'One!' and Number Three snaps his fingers, Number Three must give the Banker a toothpick, whether the Banker snapped first or not.

7 A good way for the Banker to rip off loot is to tell a story, or to start talking to one of the players and somehow work one of the numbers into the story.

8 When players lose all their loot, they are out.

9 When the Banker has ripped off all the loot, the first player to go out becomes the Banker for the next round.

Spinner!

A hundred years ago, toys were hard to come by for most kids, and the existing toys were mostly simple nonbattery-operated, nonspeaking, nonbionic, everyday toys. In those days, kids often made their own toys, like this spinner.

1 You can make the same toy today out of a big button and a piece of string about three feet long.
2 You can make a button out of cardboard if you don't have one handy. Cut the cardboard into a circle or square about two inches across.
3 With the point of a pencil, poke two holes near the center of the cardboard, about a quarter inch apart.
4 Push one end of the string through one of the holes, then back through the other hole, and then tie the two ends together.
5 If you like, paint and decorate your spinner with designs or pictures.

How to Spin the Spinner

1 Hold the string as shown in the picture, with the index fingers through the loops.
2 Push the button into the center of the two strings and give it a few turns until the strings on both sides have a few twists in them.
3 Pull out on the ends of the string. This will start the button spinning as the strings start to unwind.
4 As it begins to slow down, let your hands come together a bit, and the string will twist up again.
5 Pull the string tight again, and the button will spin in the other direction. This is a bit like learning to use a yo-yo. After a while, you should be able to keep it going *almost* forever.

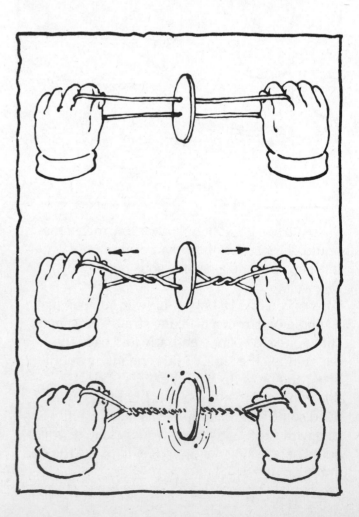

CARDBOARD

Booby Trap

PLAYERS:
2

1 First of all, you need a piece of string about three feet long. Tie one end around a wad of paper or some other small object that is easy to tie a string to (ever tried to tie a string around a coin?).
2 Next you'll need a disposable cup, preferably an empty one.
3 One player gets the cup and the other gets the string and paper ball.

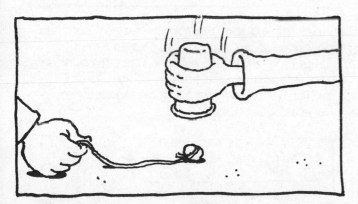

4 Put the paper ball in the middle, between the two players.
5 The player with the cup holds it four or five inches above the paper ball, but no closer! The cup person tries to trap the paper ball under the cup before the other player can pull it to safety.
6 When the ball has been trapped five times, players switch places and start a new round.
7 No fair catching the string! The ball must be under the cup to be 'trapped.'

Rubbings

Have you ever seen rubbings of tombstones, brass plaques or other monuments? To produce these beautiful rubbings, the 'rubbers' lay a sheet of paper over what they wish to copy, then rub the paper with a special large wax crayon. The crayon picks up only the raised parts of the stone or brass.

1 If you have a soft lead pencil or a crayon, as well as a supply of paper, you are nearly set to produce some rubbings of your own. All that you need now are some things to make rubbings of! You may already know that you can make rubbings of coins, but what you may not know is that you can also use leaves, cloth, sandpaper, string, the grill of your radio, etc. In short, anything that's fairly flat with some kind of texture.

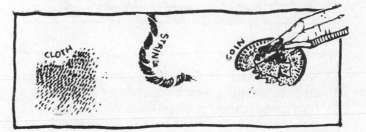

2 Lay the thing to be 'rubbed' on a hard flat surface, lay a sheet of paper over top, and carefully rub over the paper with the side of the pencil lead or with a crayon. Don't press too hard. Experiment with other things, like the tread of your shoe, textured plastic, different kinds of plants and bottle caps (a rubbing of a bottle cap looks like a sun or a flower).
3 After you have tried out a few different things, and maybe made a collection of rubbings of all the different leaves you can find, try using all the different textures you've discovered to build up a whole picture. You could use a cloth texture for the ground in a landscape, and use leaves as trees, etc. Or you could arrange a piece of string into a picture, and make a rubbing of that. The possibilities are unlimited.

DEALING WITH A CARD

Calling All Sharks

Wild as the wind and dressed like a fool, the Joker nevertheless always appears in the best of company. He can be found rubbing shoulders with royalty – kings and queens and jacks.

He has been found as far away as China and Korea, on the long narrow playing cards used there. He is even seen on the circular cards used in India.

Master of many disguises, he appears in the Tarot deck (usually used for cartomancy, or fortune-telling with cards) dressed like a gypsy vagabond and is called the Fool, but he is still the same old Joker.

In all these decks, the Joker is the zero card. He has no number and not even a suit! He is the impetuous wanderer who no one can count on. For this reason, he is left out of most games, which certainly shows a lack of respect for someone as old as he is.

He was first seen with a pack of Chinese cards about a thousand years ago. Sometime in the late fourteenth century, the Joker got itchy feet and traveled to Europe, where card games caught on like the plague.

Things got so bad that by the fifteenth century, no one would put down his hand long enough to plough the fields or do the dishes. In many countries, cards, also known as the Devil's Picture Book, were declared illegal.

In those days, as today, there were many different kinds of card decks. Italians still play some games with the Tarot deck, and others with a deck that has money, swords, cups and batons as suits instead of hearts, diamonds, clubs and spades. In Switzerland, some decks still have shield, acorn, bell and flower suits.

The suits may have originally stood for the different levels of society - diamonds for merchants, hearts for priests, spades (from the Spanish word for spear) for soldiers and clubs for peasants.

The Joker, or Fool, is the card that represents everyone, on every level of society. Wherever and whenever he appears, from the noisy gambling casinos to the quiet game of Cheat with friends, the Joker is a card. We should deal with him!

Make Your Own

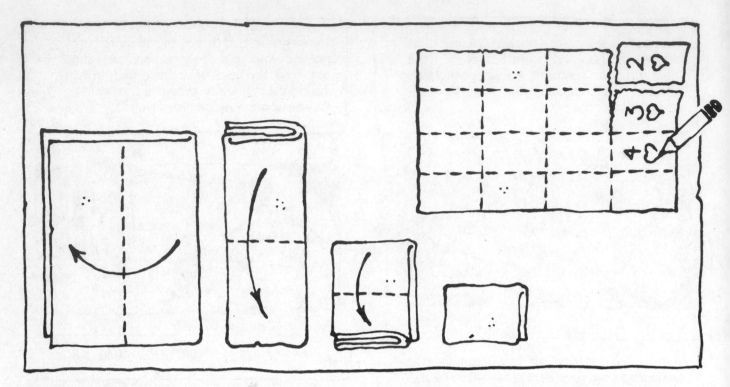

If you don't have a pack of playing cards, don't despair. Even if you only have a pencil and paper, you can do what shipwrecked castaways have been doing since there were ships and cards – namely, make your own!

In the modern deck there are 52 cards (not counting the Joker, of course). In some older European decks there were 56 cards, and there were as many as 78 in the Tarot pack. In India, decks usually have about 120 cards, but one type of deck contains 320! That's enough for over 40 people to play Old Maid with the same deck!

If you are making your own deck of cards, the games in this chapter are usually played with the modern deck – four different suits (hearts, clubs, diamonds and spades) with thirteen cards in each (Ace to ten and jack, queen and king). This makes a total of 52 cards.

1 Fold four ordinary-sized sheets of paper, as shown in the picture.

2 Unfold again and cut along the creases with scissors.

3 This will give you 16 even-sized cards per sheet of paper, or 64 cards in all, more than enough to cover for rips and mistakes.

4 Count out four piles of 13 cards each. These are the four different suits. You don't have to use hearts, clubs, diamonds and spades for suits if you don't want to. You can make up your own symbols! Like apples, hotdogs, sneakers and dollars. Or squares, circles, triangles and stars. Or whatever.

5 For each suit of 13 cards, number ten of them from Ace to ten, and mark the other three as jack, queen and king. If you like, you can decorate these cards with designs, or just write on the numbers and suits.

6 One thing to remember when you make your own cards is that the backs of the cards all have to look the same, or you will be able to tell which card is which, after a while, just by looking at the back!

Old Maid

PLAYERS:
2 TO 10

1 The object of Old Maid is to make pairs of cards, and not to be the player left with the last card, the 'Old Maid.'
2 The dealer throws away one queen from the deck and deals out all the rest of the cards one at a time, face down, to each player until the whole deck is dealt.
3 Players look at their hands and take out any pairs of cards with the same numbers on them. If they have three cards with the same number, they can only take out two of them.
4 The dealer turns to the player on his or her left and holds out his cards, *face down*. The other player takes one card from them, throws away any pair, or puts the card in his hand and then offers his cards to the player on his left, and so on.
5 The game continues like this until there is only one card left that has not been made into a pair. This is the odd queen. The player who has this card is the Old Maid and can't score. All the other players score one point for every pair they have collected.

Thirty-one

PLAYERS:
2 TO 10

1 The object of the game is to have three cards of the same suit that add up to 31 or to be the player with the highest hand. Ace counts as 11, face cards 10, all others as their face value.
2 The dealer deals three cards face down to each player, turns one card face up in the middle of the table, and puts the rest of the deck face down beside it.
3 Players take turns picking up the top card from either pile, then discarding any one of their cards face up onto the face-up pile. Players collect high-ranking cards of one suit, trying to get three that add up to 31, or as close to it as possible.
4 Players at their turn *must* pick up a card and discard a card. You can only have three cards in your hand.
5 If a player has 31 (an Ace and two ten-value cards), he knocks on the table. This means that all the other players get one more turn, and then all the players turn up their cards.
6 If no one else gets 31, the player who knocked wins the round and scores a point. If, however, another player gets 31 in the round after the knock, *that* player wins and the player who knocked loses.
7 If two players other than the one who knocked both get 31, the player who got it first wins.
8 At any time, a player can 'bluff' or pretend, and knock without having 31. You can do this if you have three cards of the same suit and if you think your total will beat out everyone else's. If another player's score is the same, higher or if somebody else gets 31, you lose.

Cheat

PLACE:

PLAYERS:
2 TO 13

Hats off to the genius who invented Cheat. It's a brilliant game that allows us to get the desire to cheat out of our systems. You know, in some countries, cheating itself is not considered so bad. In fact, you are thought of as quite clever if you can get away with it, but heaven help the cheater who gets caught in the act!

1 One pack of cards is enough for up to seven players, but for more than that shuffle two decks together.

2 The object of the game is to be the first player to get rid of all your cards.

3 The dealer deals the cards one at a time, face down to each player until one card is left. This card is turned face up in the middle of the table.

4 Players each look at their cards. Try to sort your cards into the four suits, as it is the suit and not the number of the cards that's important in this game.

5 Players take turns laying one card at a time *face down* on top of the card on the table.

6 The cards you lay down are *supposed* to be the same as the one on the table, but in actual fact, you can lay down any kind of card you like. But keep a straight face!

7 If at any time a player suspects that another player has put down a card that is not the right suit, he says, 'Cheat!' The other player must then turn over the card he just played.

8 If it is *not* the right suit (if he 'cheated') the player must pick up *all* the cards on the table and put them in his hand.

9 If the player who called 'Cheat' is wrong (if the last player *didn't* cheat), *he* must pick up all the cards!

10 The player who picks up all the cards must place a new card of a *different* suit face up on the table, and play continues as before.

11 The first player to get rid of all the cards in his hand is the winner.

Crazy Eights

PLAYERS:
2 TO 5

In this card game, the eights are wild. Absolutely and utterly crazy. The jacks are kind of strange too!

1 The object of the game is to be the first player to get rid of all your cards.

2 The dealer deals eight cards face down to each player, puts one card face up in the middle of the table and puts the rest of the deck face down beside it.

3 Players take turns putting one card face up on the face-up card. The cards played must be of the same suit as the first card.

4 If you can't play a card of the same suit as the cards on the face-up pile, you must pick up one from the other pile, and your turn passes to the next player.

5 You can change the suit by playing a card with the same value, or number, as the last card played. For instance, if the last card played was a six of spades, you can play a six of another suit on top, which changes the suit being played to the suit of the new six. All cards played after this must be of the new suit, until it is changed again.

6 Some of the cards are special. If you put down a jack, you can put down another card of the same suit on top, thus playing two cards on one turn. If you have two jacks, you can put the second jack on top of the first (if the first one is playable) and then a card of the same suit as the second jack, on top of it. (Sounds complicated doesn't it?) This means that you have changed the suit being played, as well as playing three cards at one turn!

7 Another way to change the suit being played is to play an eight. Since eights are wild, you can change the suit to anything you want.

8 There are still a few more special cards. If you play a two, the player next to you must pick up two cards, then play.

9 If you play the queen of spades, the player next to you must pick up *four* cards.

10 If the pick-up pile runs out of cards, shuffle the face-up pile, turn it over, and use it for the pick-up pile.

11 The first player to run out of cards in his hand is the winner!

This Means War!!

PLASYERS:
2 TO 8

In some games, the Ace is the highest card, and in some games it is the lowest card. In the official rules for this game, the Ace is high!

1 The object of War is to win all the cards in the deck.

2 The dealer deals out the whole deck face down, one card at a time to each player, until all the cards are dealt

3 Players must not look at their cards, but put them in one pile face down in front of them.

4 At the same time, all the players turn over the top card from their pile

5 The highest card wins. The player with the highest card picks up the other players' turned-up cards and puts them face down on the bottom of his own stack.

6 If two or three of the cards on the table are the same rank (two kings, two 2s, or whatever), the players with those cards cover their own card with three more cards *face down* and then one more face up. The person with the highest card up wins all the cards just played and puts them on the bottom of his pile.

7 If the second face-up cards are the same again the players put down three more face down and one more face up, the winner taking all cards.

8 If you have no more cards to put down, you are out.

9 The first person to get all the cards is the winner.

Beggar My Neighbor

PLAYERS:
2 OR 3

1 The object of the game, as in War, is to win all the cards.

2 The dealer deals out the cards, one at a time and face down, to each player until all the cards are dealt.

3 Players *do not* look at their cards but hold them in one pile, face down.

4 Players take turns putting one card, face up, in the center of the table on one pile.

5 When one of the players turns up a jack, queen, king or Ace, the next player has to pay one or more 'penalty' cards (like a five). The person who played the face card picks up all the cards in the center of the table, shuffles them and puts them on the bottom of his pile.

6 These are the penalties: if one player puts down a jack, the next player must put down one card; a queen, two cards; a king, three cards; and an Ace, four cards!

7 If you turn up a face card when you are playing your penalty cards, you stop, and the player next to *you* must pay the penalty for it and *you* get to pick up all the cards.

8 If this second player puts down a face card when he is paying his penalty, the third player must pay the penalty, and the second player wins the cards. Sometimes this can go on and on, until finally one player pays his full penalty without playing a face card. Then the last person who played a face card wins the pile of cards.

9 If a player runs out of cards to play in his turn, he may 'borrow' one card from the bottom of the center pile and can continue to do so until he either wins or loses.

10 The last person left in the game wins.

Try Patience

PLAYERS:
1

Patience, besides being a virtue, is the name for a group of card games for one player. There are hundreds of different kinds of Patience (also known as Solitaire), and lonely card sharks are probably thinking up new ones all the time.

This is a very simple version.

1 Go through the deck and take out all cards lower than seven, leaving in the Aces.
2 Shuffle the rest of the cards and deal them out one at a time face up, at the same time saying 'Seven, eight, nine, ten, jack, queen, king, Ace....' Say one word for each card you lay down.
3 After you have laid down the first eight cards, go through the numbers again.
4 If the card you lay down is the same as the name you call out, remove that card from the pile.
5 The object of the game is to get rid of all the cards in this way.
6 When you have gone through the deck once, shuffle the cards and start again, but start the sequence where you left off. For example, if you say 'jack' as you put down the last card, you shuffle the cards, put the first one down, and say 'queen.'
7 If at any time you go through the deck once without taking out at least one card, you lose and must start again with all the cards. This is true even if your deck has only three or four cards left in it.

Rudi's Patience

PLAYERS:
1

If playing the first kind of Patience didn't try your patience to the breaking point, have a go at this kind of Patience.

1 Take the four Aces out of the deck and put them down, side by side, face up. Shuffle the rest of the deck.
2 The object of the game is to get a row of cards in the order two, three, four, five, six, seven, eight, nine, ten, jack, queen, king, on top of each Ace, ignoring suits.
3 Deal cards one at a time off the top of the deck. If they fit in with any sequence already started on the Aces, place them there. If they don't, place them face up on *any one* of four 'waste' piles at the bottom.
4 At any time, the top card of any waste pile can be played.
5 For example, the picture shows a game in progress. The first row is almost finished, and the player can add the nine, ten and jack from the top of the waste piles. If there are any cards just under these that fit in with any sequence, they can be used once they are exposed.
6 If you complete all four rows in order from Ace to king, you win!

RADIO MANIA

Don't Touch That Dial!

Somewhere around the end of the last century, folks began to invent the radio. People with names like Hughes, Hertz, Lodge and Marconi began fooling around with coils, tubes and wires - sending noise, static, squawks and whistles across their labs or down the street, by means of radio waves! Science triumphs again!

EUREKA!

What the world didn't know was that a New York inventor named Nikola Tesla and a Kentucky farmer named Nathan Stubblefield had both beat the whole bunch to the draw and had sent voice and music over radio waves back before 1892!

In 1901, Marconi succeeded in sending a signal across the Atlantic - three short dots of static. Soon Marconi's radio equipment was being used on ships for sending messages to shore and to each other using Morse Code.

In 1906, ship radio operators were surprised to hear actual voices and music in their headphones instead of the usual dots and dashes! The signal was generated from Massachusetts by a Canadian inventor named Fessenden, and it was almost the first time that the human voice and music had traveled the radio waves.

The great Age of Radio had begun. Soon, nearly everyone was tuning into the great old adventure and comedy shows, music, commercials, soap operas, commercials, news of war and disaster and commercials in the comfort of their own homes, and a little later on in cars.

Some people say that radio has never been as good as in those old golden days in the 1930s. This is your chance to prove them wrong! Start your own radio station!

Make up your own adventure and comedy shows, music, soap operas, commercials and news! The games in this chapter will give you all kinds of suggestions, and you probably have lots of great ideas of your own.

If you have a cassette recorder, you and your friends could make tapes of your zany radio shows – save as many as you can – they'll be great to listen to in later years.

If you want to make some musical instruments, you'll need some scrap materials; otherwise, if you have a voice, you are fully dressed for radio!

Homemade Music

If you did some of the activities in the Scrap Happy chapter, then you know the true value of things like disposable cups, straws, bottle caps and other so-called 'litter.' If you are feeling musical and can lay your hands on some scrap, try making some of these great instruments. If you get enough people together, you can form an honest-to-goodness jug band.

Cup Banjo

The Jug

1 What would a jug band be without an honest-to-goodness jug? Any old pop bottle makes a good jug.
2 Put the top of the bottle against your bottom lip and blow across the opening. If you hold the bottle at the correct angle, music will appear! This makes good background music for the banjo and the 'woodwinds.'

1 If you are lucky enough to find a rubber band, you have the basic part for any kind of stringed instrument you want to make. Just strumming the elastic by itself doesn't make much of a noise. You need something to *amplify* the sound (make it louder).
2 Wrap the elastic around a cup as shown in the drawing and strum on the part that crosses the mouth of the cup. Now *that's* music!

3 Put a pencil or your finger under the elastic on the side of the cup. As you pull it away from the side of the cup, the sound of the notes will change, and you'll find that you can play a whole range of sounds.

Saxa-phony

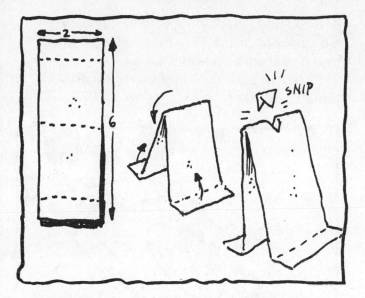

1 This saxa-phony is as easy to make as it is to play, and that's easy! Its range of sound is limited (it only produces one note, but oh, what a note!), but it is good for filling in to give that 'Big Band' sound.

2 To make it, cut a strip of paper about six inches long and two or three wide.

3 Fold it in half in the middle and fold up the two ends as shown in the picture.

4 Cut out a small V in the middle fold, and your saxa-phony is finished.

5 To play it, hold it in your hand as shown, and place the two folded-up flaps against your lips.

6 Blow through, and the most beautiful sound will issue forth, not unlike the lonely evening call of the lovesick duckbilled platypus.

Tambourine

1 To play the tambourine, you have to have rhythm, you got to have beat, and you must have money! What? Why money you ask? Because money is what this tambourine is made of, that's why. Yep, nothing beats the sound of cold, hard cash hitting more cold, hard cash.

2 To make this tambourine, just reach into your pocket or purse, pull out a handful of any kind of coins, cup both hands together with the coins inside and shake them for all you're worth!

3 The job of the tambourine is to lay down the beat that the other instruments play to. But remember, be careful with your new tambourine, it's a valuable instrument!

Percussion

1 All you need to make this instrument is one good hand and one good mouth. It's easier if they are both your own.

2 Open your mouth without showing your teeth, and lightly hit your mouth with the fingers of your hand, which are held together, straight out.

3 This looks like you are performing an Apache war whoop without the whoop. This will make a sort of 'bip, bop' sound that changes as you open and close your mouth.

Marimbas

1 *Aye Yi Yi!* Having a good marimba player in your band can really snazz up your sound. The marimbas are a lot like the tambourine described earlier, but the sound is much louder and deeper.
2 Take a disposable cup, with the lid if you have it (if you don't, you can cover the top with your hand).

3 Put a few small coins or pebbles or bottle caps in the cup. Put the lid on or cover the cup.
4 Shake well. The traditional sound is three short shakes, then pause, three short shakes, then pause, and so on, but let the music move you.

Kandy Kazoo

1 If you find one of those little candy boxes with a cellophane 'window' in the front, you've just found yourself a kandy kazoo!
2 Open one end of the box, cover it with your mouth, and blow.

3 Play it the same way you whistle, in short and long and hard and soft bursts of air. To vary the sound even more, try squeezing the sides of the box in and out.

Organically Grown Trumpet

1 Like the jug, the saxa-phony and the kandy kazoo, the O.G. trumpet is a wind instrument, because your wind is what makes the sound.
2 It's made from a single piece of crabgrass held between your two thumbs as shown in the drawings.

3 The piece of grass should be flat, with the edge toward you, and held tightly between the top and base of your thumbs.
4 When you blow just right in the opening between your thumbs, the most bee-yutiful high-pitched squawk comes forth. Blow harder and lighter to change the sound.

Drums

1 Drums have been a big favorite for giving music 'punch' since the days of cave living.
2 Almost anything can be used for a drum – a suitcase, a book, an upside-down pot or box, or whatever.

3 Things that are hard and hollow produce a lower, louder sound than anything else.
4 One thing to watch out for – don't play the drums too loud or you will drown out the other players.

Vocals

Of course, just instruments do not a jug band make. Every good jug band needs a little bit of the human voice to lend meaning to the music. You can write your own songs, make them up as you go along or sing ones that you already know. When in doubt, hum or whistle.

Got your instruments all tuned up? Quiet on the set – 1,2,3,4!

Poison Penny

PLAYERS:
4 OR MORE

If you have made some of the musical instruments described in the last game, Poison Penny is the perfect game to try them out on.

1 Each person gets a chance to act as a soloist.
2 The soloist closes his or her eyes and plays some music – any kind of music will do – while the other players pass a penny from hand to hand, around in a circle.
3 When the music stops, the person left holding the Poison Penny becomes the soloist, and the former soloist takes his place in the circle.

4 If the penny is in between two players, being passed from hand to hand when the music stops, it doesn't count as 'poison.' Neither player has to leave the circle. Instead, the soloist starts again and tries to trap someone else.

Ten Tongue-tanglers

'Howdy howdy howdy!! This is Carry LaRock for WHUH Radio, bringin' you some of the hits most of the time, most of the hits some of the time and all of the hits none of the time!!'

Good DJs have to be able to talk clearly and *fast*, without saying anything at all. Practice these tongue-tanglers faithfully, and before you know it, you'll have a voice like honey and a tongue like rubber.

Start out with a few of these 'simple' ones. Say each of these ten times:

- Unique New York
- Rubber baby buggy bumpers
- A proper copper coffee pot
- A stewed sow's snout
- Three gray geese in a green field grazing

Is your voice beginning to sound like that smooth baritone? Okay, finish off your warming-up session with these next twisters:

A woman to her son did utter
Go, my son, and shut the shutter.
The shutter's shut, the son did mutter,
I cannot shut it any shutter!

There's no need to light a nightlight
On a light night like tonight
For a night-light's a slight light
On a light night like tonight.

A tutor who tooted the flute
Tried to tutor two tooters to toot,
Said the two to the tutor
Is it harder to toot
Or to tutor two tooters to toot?

Of all the felt I ever felt,
I never felt a piece of felt
That felt the same as that felt felt
When I first felt the felt of that felt hat.

How much wood could a woodchuck chuck
If a woodchuck could chuck wood?

The Poetry Hour

Put a little culture in your radio programing for your highbrow listeners and start a Poetry Hour show! Give a chance to the budding bards in your midst to read their own verse out loud, or try some of the examples below.

'Tis Midnight

'Tis midnight, and the setting sun
Is slowly rising in the west;
The rapid rivers slowly run,
The frog is on his downy nest.
The pensive goat and sportive cow,
Hilarious, leap from bough to bough.

Dumb Boids

Toity poible boids,
Sittin on da coib
Choipin and a boipin
An eatin doity woims.

The Ill-fated Promenade

Three young rats with black felt hats,
Three young ducks with white straw flats,
Three young dogs with curling tails,
Three young cats with demi-veils,
Went out to walk with two young pigs
In satin vests and sorrel wigs;
But suddenly it chanced to rain,
And so they all went home again.

Mary's Song

Mary went down to Grandpa's farm,
The billy goat chased her around the barn.
Chased her up the sycamore tree,
And this is the song she sang to me:
'I like coffee, I like tea,
I like the boys and the boys like me!'

Singing in Rounds

If you have never sung in rounds before, you have been missing out on one of the great things that life has to offer.

The basic idea is this:

1 One person starts singing the song.

2 When he has finished singing the first line, he keeps going, but the next person starts singing the first line when the first person is starting on the second line.

3 When the second person is starting on the second line, the third person starts singing the first line, and so on, until everyone is singing a different line.

4 Here are the words for three of the most popular round songs, with the English words for Frère Jacques.

Three blind mice, three blind mice.
See how they run, see how they run.
They all ran after the farmer's wife,
She cut off their tails with a butcher knife!
Did you ever see such a sight in your life,
As three blind mice?

Row, row, row your boat
Gently down the stream.
Merrily, merrily, merrily, merrily,
Life is but a dream.

Frère Jacques, Frère Jacques,
Dormez-vous? Dormez-vous?
Sonnez les matines, sonnez les matines,
Ding dang dong! Ding dang dong!

Are you sleeping? Are you sleeping?
Brother John, Brother John,
Morning bells are ringing, morning bells are ringing.
Ding dang dong! Ding dang dong!

5 If you are singing Frère Jacques, you could have every second singer singing the English version.

You may find singing like this very difficult at first, but after you get used to it, it's the most natural thing in the world.

GAMES FOR ONE TEAM

Group Effort

Now, there's nothing wrong with a good honest game played by the rules, but we all know that most games are just friendly wars, and sometimes everyone gets the feeling that he would rather just relax for a while and have fun, without having to worry about the score sheet.

YOUR MOVE!!

How would you like to leave all this silly competition behind? How would you like to play games that have never heard of things like 'winning' or 'losing?' How would you like to play <u>with</u> your friends instead of <u>against</u> them?

The games in this chapter are specially designed with this in mind. There are no winners, and so there are also no losers. There is only one team of friends with one object in mind: having fun!

A Likely Story

PLAYERS:
2 OR MORE

This game is a good test of your memory and imagination.

1 One of the players makes a list of about six or eight objects, then reads it out loud, slowly. The list is then hidden.

2 The first player makes up one sentence, using the first object on the list.

3 The second player repeats the first player's sentence and then makes up a new sentence that carries on the story and also uses the second object on the list.

4 The third player repeats the first two sentences, then adds a new one, using the third object on the list.

5 The story travels around the circle of players in this way, each player repeating all the previous sentences, then adding on a new one that uses the next object on the list.

6 If one player makes a mistake, you have to start over again from the very beginning.

7 For instance, if your list of objects looked like this: cage, bird, tree, rabbit, bridge, telephone, train, city, then your finished story might go something like this:

Once upon a time, there was a beautiful gold and silver cage covered in jewels.

In this cage lived a beautiful bird.

One day the bird escaped and flew to a nearby tree.

Under the tree sat a rabbit.

The rabbit saw the bird and walked over a bridge.

He went to a telephone to phone the owners of the bird to tell them where it was hiding out.

'You rat fink!' screeched the bird, and hopped onto a passing freight train.

It was last seen heading east for the nearest city.

THEN what happened?? YOU tell ME!

Beep

PLAYERS:
2 OR MORE

1 The players count in a circle.

2 The first player says 'one,' the second player says 'two,' the third player says 'three,' and so on.

3 Sounds pretty easy so far. But whenever any player comes to the number seven, or any multiple of seven (14, 21, 28, 35, 42, 49, etc.) or even a number with seven in it (17, 27, 37, 77…), instead of saying one of those dirty 'seven' numbers, he or she must say 'BEEP!' instead.

4 If you forget to say Beep, everyone must go right back to the beginning and start counting over again.

5 The object of the game is to try to count up to 100 without anyone making a single mistake.

6 Here's how the first part of the counting should go: 1, 2, 3, 4, 5, 6, beep, 8, 9, 10, 11, 12, 13, beep, 15, 16, beep, and so on. Remember your seven-times table!

Tom, Dick & Harry

PLAYERS:
2 OR MORE

Tom, Dick and Harry is a game named after its inventors, Tom, Dick, and last but not least, Harry. It's a lot like Beep, but it's much more complicated.

1 Like Beep, the players count in a circle, each one saying one number at a time.

2 In this game you can say seven as often as you want, but instead of saying one, you must say Tom, instead of saying two, you must say Dick, and instead of saying three you say Harry.

3 When you come to ten you say Tom-zero, for 11 you say Tom-Tom, and the number 31 is Harry-Tom.

4 The first bit of counting goes like this: Tom, Dick, Harry, 4, 5, 6, 7, 8, 9, Tom-zero, Tom-Tom, Tom-Dick, Tom-Harry, Tom-4, etc.

Exquisite Corpses

PLACES:
2 OR MORE

Exquisite Corpses sounds like the name for some kind of weird horror movie, but in actual fact it is the name of a hilarious game that a few of you are probably familiar with.

1 The first player takes a piece of paper and at the top draws the head of a figure, keeping the drawing hidden from the other players.
2 He or she folds the paper over, so that just a little part of the neck can be seen, and passes the paper to the next player.

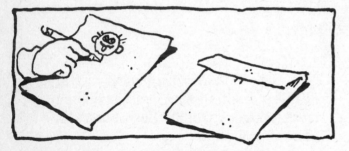

3 The next player draws the top half of the mystery figure's body, without looking to see what the head looks like. He then folds the paper over, so that none of the other players can see what has been drawn, and passes the folded paper to the next player, who does the legs, and so on.
4 When the last player has finished drawing the feet, open the paper and have a look at the strange creature your imaginations have hatched.

One-liners

PLAYERS:
2 OR MORE

An Exquisite Corpse Story

Working with other people on the job of making up stories can be fun. You see the story start moving in one direction, and next thing you know, it has taken off in every direction at once. Things start happening that you would never have thought possible. This is also fun to do with a tape recorder so you can play it back.

1 The first player starts the story by saying one sentence – any sentence that comes to mind.
2 Each player then takes turns adding one more sentence at a time.
3 By the time the third player has added a sentence, a general story line should begin to show up.
4 If you had the time, the story could go on forever. But if you want to make the game more difficult, make a rule that each player can only say a total of three sentences, and that the last three sentences of the story must tie it up somehow and end the story, leaving no loose ends.

Sound Effects

PLERS:
3 OR MORE

1 Each player should think of what kind of animal he would like to be, if he could, and what kind of noise that animal makes.

2 Have one of the players who is good at storytelling make up a story that tells the adventures of all the animals that the other players have chosen to imitate. You could all take turns at this part if you like, or you could work together as a group to make the story, and have one person read it.

3 Whenever the storyteller mentions the name of one of the animals, the person who is that animal must make the right animal noise. So whenever the storyteller mentions a horse, the 'horse' should whinny; and whenever a dog is mentioned, the 'dog' should bark and growl, and so on.

4 The storyteller can make all the other sound effects for the story, such as stampeding gophers, rocket blast-offs, giant's footsteps, toasters popping, train whistles, gunshots, screams, crowds cheering, and that sort of thing.

MISCELLANEOUS MAGIC

Enchanting Your Audience With String, Cards, Coins, Dice, Handkerchiefs and Numbers

Everyone knows that magic isn't <u>really</u> Magic. Magic with a capital M is a different thing altogether.

Everybody knows that all a magician does is take ordinary objects and do things with them that look totally impossible, which is exactly what a juggler, fire-eater or sword-swallower does. Or even a carpenter for that matter.

AND NOW, FOR MY NEXT TRICK...

So don't try to fool your audience into thinking that you have some kind of Magical Powers, because they know as well as you do that it's just not true. What appears to be magical mind-over-matter is merely a matter of the hand being quicker than the eye.

LOOK! MAGIC!

What any audience wants is to be entertained. They are amazed and amused by clowns, jugglers, acrobats, fire-eaters, comedians and actors, not because they think the performer is Magic, but because of the performer's skill.

Even though they know that every incredible miracle and impossible trick a magician does has some kind of perfectly good explanation, they will still be excited, mystified, bewildered, perplexed and downright baffled!

PICK A CARD, ANY CARD...

If you want to impress your friends with magic tricks, there is one thing you'll need lots of, and it isn't supernatural powers – it's practice. Practice all the tricks here alone and in front of a mirror until you can do them with your eyes closed.

Also, keep talking! Keep up a pleasant patter, try to look calm and innocent at all times and, above all, keep a straight face when you are slipping cards out of your sleeves, performing a phony shuffle or palming a coin!

There are a few other basic rules you should know before performing magic. If you are doing something secret with your left hand, look at your right hand. If you are doing something tricky with both hands, look your audience right in the eye, so that some of their attention will be distracted.

Into Thin Air!

For this trick, all you need is a coin, or some other small object. You may need to practice this a bit before you get it just right, but once you know how to do it, you will never forget.

The audience sees you holding a coin in your left hand. You then seem to pick up the coin with your right hand. But when you open your right hand, the coin just isn't there - it has disappeared into thin air! Just when the audience has given up hope of ever seeing it again, you reach up and pull the coin out from behind someone's ear!

The Secret

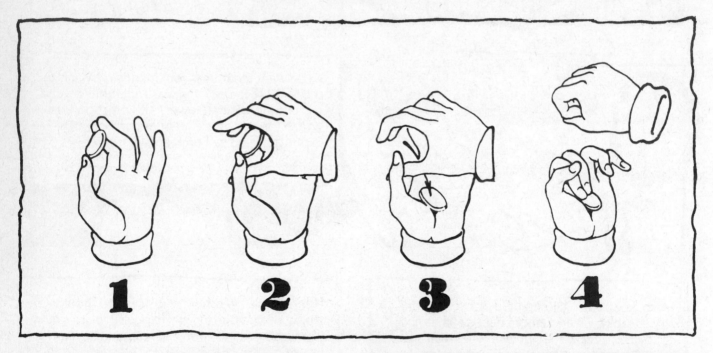

1   2   3   4

Sounds spectacular, doesn't it? If you do it quickly and well, it *is* spectacular.

1 Hold the coin between the tips of your left index finger and thumb.

2 Then, quickly and with a smooth motion, pass your right thumb under the coin as if you are going to pick it up.

3 But in actual fact, what you really do is drop the coin into the palm of your left hand!

4 Without stopping, your right hand closes as if it has just grabbed the coin. All the tricky action is hidden by the fingers of your left hand. Look at the drawings and this will be clear - just remember the picture is seen from *your* point of view.

5 Remember not to look at your hands during all this, but to look into the eyes of the audience. Otherwise, they will suspect that something tricky is going on.

6 Draw all attention at this point to your right hand, which is actually empty. Hold it up and let your left hand drop to your side.

7 Blow on your right hand and then quickly open it up. The coin's gone!

8 While your audience is goggling, quickly reach up with your left hand, and touch someone behind his ear. When you open your left hand revealing the coin, it will seem as if it came from his ear!

Feat of Strength

This is a trick that works itself; all you have to do is follow instructions.

Tell your friends that you have been studying an ancient form of meditation and that you can lock your muscles like iron.

'For instance,' you say, 'what would you think if I told you that you could not move my arm, no matter how hard you tried?' They're bound to think you're a little bit nuts, especially if they are bigger than you, but that won't help them!

The Secret

Put the palm of either hand on the top of your head and ask a volunteer to try to lift your hand off your head by *pushing* up on your arm from below. Chances are he will find it downright impossible!

Triple Dice Guess

If you pull this trick off, your friends will be totally dumbfounded.

You need three dice. For complete instructions on making dice, see the Scrap Happy chapter. It is very important that the opposite faces add up to seven!

1 You turn your back, and someone from the audience rolls the three dice and adds up the numbers on their faces. Tell him not to move or touch the dice unless you say to.

2 Then, following your instructions, he picks any two dice and adds their *bottom* faces to the total.

3 He then throws those two dice and adds the top two faces to the total.

4 Then he takes any *one* of the two dice and adds its bottom face to the total.

5 He then throws it, and adds its top face to the total. When he is finished, you turn around, look at the dice on the table for a second and tell him the total!

The Secret

Your audience may be in a state of shock after you show them the trick, but can you blame them? After all, you must admit that it's a pretty amazing trick. And it's so simple too. The total is always equal to the sum of the top faces on the dice plus 21, because opposite sides of dice always add up to seven. So you merely turn around, add up the top faces on the dice, add 21, and announce the total!

Mathementics

You don't need any practice for this trick, but it is so stupendous that your friends will be stupefied.

1 You write a number down on a piece of paper and hand it to someone from the audience, who tucks it safely away in a pocket.

2 Ask this person to write down any number between 50 and 100 on another sheet of paper.

3 Ask him to subtract a number from his number, do a couple of other simple mathematical calculations, and then look at the piece of paper you gave him at the beginning of the trick. The number on it is the same as his final result!

The Secret

This trick uses simple mathematical principles.

1 You write down any number between 1 and 50 on a scrap of paper, fold the paper and give it to your friend to put in his pocket. Let's say you pick 18.

2 Ask your friend to choose a number between 50 and 100, and to write it down on another piece of paper without letting you see it. Let's say he picks 75.

3 In your head, subtract the number *you* wrote down from 99, and ask your friend to add the result to his number.

$$99 - 18 = 81 \qquad 75 + 81 = 156$$

4 Now ask your friend to cross off the first digit of his new number (in this case, the 1 of 156), and then to add *that* digit to the result, still keeping his calculations hidden from you.

$$
\begin{array}{r}
\cancel{1}56 \\
+1 \\
\hline
57
\end{array}
$$

5 Tell your friend to subtract this new number from his original number and then to open the piece of paper you gave him in the beginning of the trick. The numbers are the same!

$$75 - 57 = 18$$

If you want to learn more number tricks, look up Abraca-algebra in the Count Me In chapter.

EUREKA! I'VE DISCOVERED A WHOLE NEW BRANCH OF MATHEMATICS!

The Hypnotized Straw

The audience sees you lay a short straw down on the table, and then start rubbing your finger around it in a circle.

'Building up a static electrical charge around the straw...' you say. Your finger circles the straw a few more times, and then you slide your finger away from it. Suddenly, to your audience's surprise, the straw rolls away, following your finger along the table top!

The Secret

It is dangerous to do this trick more than once. You may need to practice a bit, but basically it's very simple.

1 You lay the straw on the table, and begin rubbing your finger in a circle around it. Rub harder and harder, focusing all your attention on the straw.

2 Finally, after everyone else is looking intently at the straw, waiting for something to happen, rub your finger away from you along the table. At the same time, blow slightly on the straw, and it will roll along the table top, seeming to follow your finger.

3 The others will be looking so hard at the table that they will not see you blowing. Of course, if they don't know the secret, the trick won't work when your friends try it.

The Loop Escapes!

For this amazing trick all you need is a rubber band, a piece of string about two or three feet long, and a little practice. A member of the audience ties each end of the string around one of your wrists, so that you are wearing a pair of string handcuffs like the ones shown in the picture. You then take the rubber band, turn your back for a second, and when you turn to face the audience again, the rubber band is hanging from the middle of the string. Turn around again, and the loop escapes from the string again! The knots on your wrists have not been touched, and anyway, you didn't have time. How did you do it?

The Secret

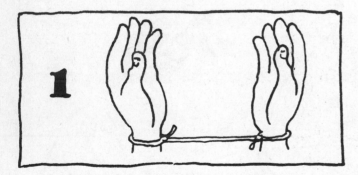

1 Your friends tie your wrists as shown, and you turn around.

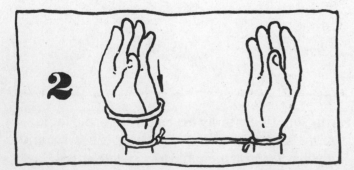

2 When your back is turned, slip the rubber band over your left hand (if you don't have a rubber band, you can use a loop made of string or ribbon, with one big impossible-to-untie knot).

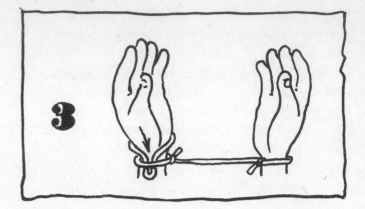

3 Slip a bit of the rubber band under the string around your wrist, and then pull the rest of it through so that the band is now below the string.

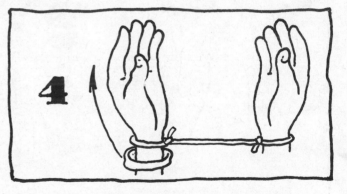

4 Pass the rubber band back over your hand, and it will be trapped in the middle of the string!

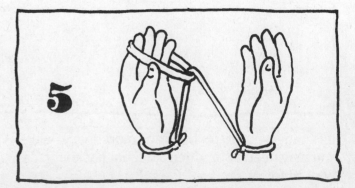

5 Take the loop off by doing the whole thing backward.

Before you take the string handcuffs off your wrists, have a look at the next trick.

Making Things Worse

This is an old trick and, if done well, a good trick. A member of the audience ties your hands in a pair of string handcuffs like the ones used in the last trick. (If you still have them on from the last trick, use them!) Tell the audience you are going to escape from these 'chains.' You turn your back on them for no more than a few seconds, certainly not enough time to untie your handcuffs, and when you turn back to face them again, there is a series of knots in the middle of the string! You have not escaped. You have only made things worse!

The Secret

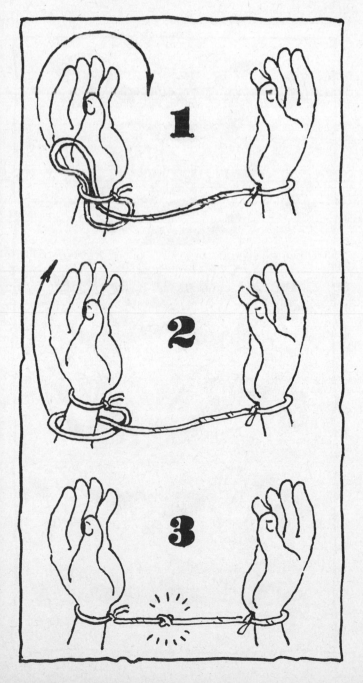

It might take everyone a while to realize that it's impossible for those knots to be there, right in the middle of the string like that. Or at least it *seems* impossible. It's actually the same principle that was used in the last trick that makes this trick work.

1 When you turn your back, take the center of the string and push it under the loop around your left wrist from below, as shown in the first drawing.

2 Pass the new loop over your left hand, and then pull it from under the loop around your wrist, so that it now looks like the second drawing.

3 If you pull this loop off your left hand, it will form an overhand knot in the center of the string.

4 With practice, you can do as many of these as you want in a few seconds, and the entire audience will be at a loss as to how you did it. Pretend that you don't know either, and ask for some help to get free!

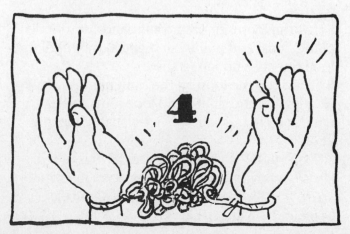

Now You See It...

And now you don't! This trick is a little complicated to learn, but it's actually quite simple once you get the hang of it. You can do it with string or rope, but it is most impressive if you use a long silk scarf.

Ask a member of the audience to try to tie a knot in the scarf without letting go of the ends. After they have tried and failed, take hold of the ends of the silk scarf, and, without letting go once, you tie a big knot in the center. Blow on the knot, and it disappears!

The Secret

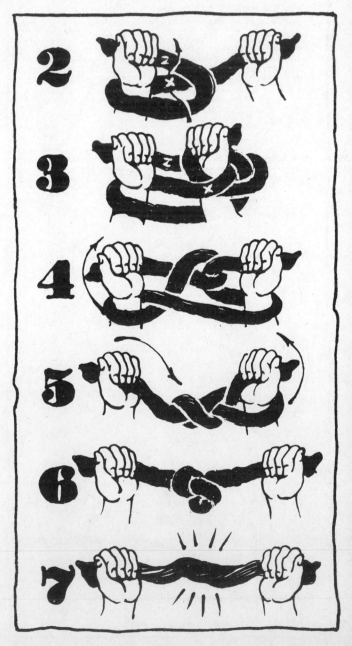

Before you can do this trick well, you'll need to practice.

1 Hold the scarf in both hands as shown in the first drawing.

2 Bring your right hand over and around your left hand so that a loop is formed on your left wrist, as shown in the second drawing.

3 Still holding both ends, put your right hand into the loop from above, under the part marked X, and over the part marked Z.

4 When you move your hands apart, you will have a twisted mass of silk scarf wrapped around them that looks a little like the fourth picture.

5 Let the loop slip off the left hand (don't let go of the end!) and pull the left end slowly until the loop bunches up into a knot.

6 Then slip the loop off the right hand, and pull slowly until the right-hand loop joins the left-hand loop in the center in a big, nasty-looking knot.

7 Don't pull too hard, because this isn't a real knot, it's an imposter! If you blow on it and pull sharply on both ends of the scarf, it will disappear! (The knot, that is.)

A Useful Knot

This is the kind of knot that is nice to have around. Not only is it very easy to tie, but it knows how to untie itself!

The Secret

You can use string, rope or a handkerchief for this trick, but a silk scarf works best.

1 Hold one end of the scarf, or whatever, in each hand.

2 Twist the ends around each other once, then hold them in the same hands again. See the first drawing.

3 Next, tie one knot above this twist, and pull on the ends and sides of the scarf at once, tightening the knot.

4 This knot will hold together well enough, but if you take hold of one end of the scarf and shake it hard once or twice, the knot will seem to melt!

Shuffle Sorcery

The Trick Shuffle can be done as a trick by itself as well. You tell a spectator to pick a card, any card. You cut the deck, and he puts his card back on top of the bottom pile. You put the two piles together again, shuffle the cards well and then proceed to pull his card from the top of the deck!

The Secret

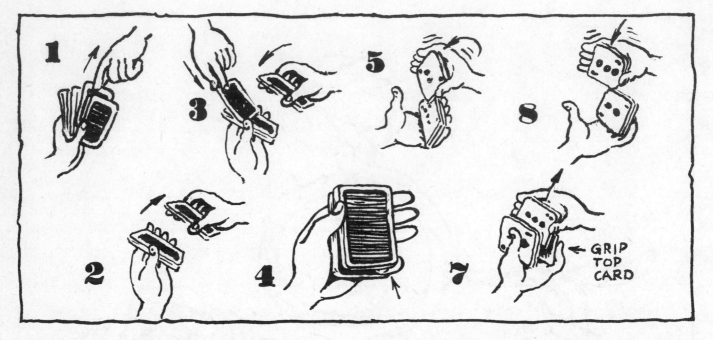

1 Your friend takes any card and looks at it.

2 Cut the deck, then with your right hand lift up about half the pile of cards.

3 Your friend puts his card *face down* on top of the pile in your left hand, and you put the pile in your right hand down on top of that.

4 But just before the top pile hits the bottom pile, curl the tip of your left little finger over the top of the bottom pile. If you do this quickly enough, and hold the deck tightly, the spectator will not suspect a thing; he will think that his card is lost somewhere in the middle of the deck, while in actual fact your little finger marks exactly where it is!

5 Now, as you start shuffling, lift the whole top pile off from above your little finger, and shuffle it to the bottom of the pile.

6 The chosen card should now be on the top of the deck.

7 This is where the actual Trick Shuffle comes into play. Pull on the top part of the deck as if you were going to perform a normal shuffle, but keep your fingers pressed lightly against the top card.

8 As you pull up on the top half of the deck, the top card will secretly slip off, held by the pressure of your fingers, and will stay in place.

9 You can keep doing what looks like a normal shuffle, but the top card is always the same one!

10 After you have 'shuffled' for a few seconds, quickly flip over the top card and show it to your friend. 'Recognize this card?' you innocently ask, and the audience is astounded. Put it back down again, shuffle for a few more minutes, and there it is again! The Trick Shuffle is so easy to do that the spectators will never suspect a thing!

Triple Flip

This trick is so easy to perform that it is hard to believe people are always amazed by it!

What happens is this: you shuffle the deck, lay it on the table, and ask someone to cut it into three piles without further shuffling. Suddenly, you call out the names of the three top cards, *before* you pick each of them up. And when you lay them down on the table, sure enough, they are the ones you called out!

The Secret

1 You won't need the Trick Shuffle (the last trick) to do this one, but you do need to get a look at the top card on the deck. This is fairly easy to do if you are the one to shuffle. Pretend that you are straightening the edges of the deck, and let the top card fall back slightly so you can get a look at it. Do this quickly and without pausing.

2 Put the deck on the table and ask someone to cut it into three piles without shuffling. Keep track of which pile has the top card on it.

3 Call out the name of the card that you secretly know about, but lift up a card from a *different pile.* Look at it, but don't show it to the audience just yet.

4 Now call out the name of the card you just picked up, and lift up the other unknown top card from the second pile.

5 Call out the name of this card, and lift up the final top card, the one that you know about.

6 The last card you picked up was actually the first one you called out, but don't let the audience know this! If you lay the cards down one at a time in the order you called them, no one will suspect a thing.

Pocket Pick

No, this is not a lesson on the age-old art of picking pockets. It's a spectacular magic trick that uses a pocket, as well as a deck of cards.

You ask a member of the audience to pick a card, any card; to look at it; and to memorize it without letting you see it. He puts his card back in the deck, and you 'shuffle' it. Now you need another person with an easy-to-reach pocket. A shirt or coat pocket works best. You put the deck of cards in the pocket and have the first person blindfold you (or just close your eyes tightly). Have one of the people direct your hand to the pocket, and then, with one lightning-fast swoop, you pull out a card! When the dust has cleared, the audience sees that it is the card chosen by the first person!

The Secret

chosen card

This is really nothing other than a fancy way to show off the Trick Shuffle that you learned one or two tricks ago.

1 Using the Trick Shuffle, you make sure that the chosen card is on top of the deck.

2 When you put the deck into the pocket, make sure that you know which way it is facing. (The deck, not the pocket.)

3 When you reach in, it will be easy, blindfold and all, to find the top of the deck and to pull out the chosen card. To the audience, it seems as if you have just reached in and pulled out any old card, especially if you tell them that this is what you are going to do.

Meet the Count

The standard card trick opening: a member of the audience picks a card, looks at it and puts it back in the deck. You shuffle the cards calmly, not saying a word. Then you start counting cards one at a time off the top of the deck, asking the person who picked the card to tell you when to stop. When he tells you to stop, you put the pile of cards back on top of the deck, hand it to him, and ask him to count off the same number of cards in the same way. He does so. 'What was your card?' you ask innocently. He tells you, and when you turn over the last card that he counted out, there it is!

The Secret

...12, 13, 14..

Stop!

put back on top of deck

..14.

chosen card

Like the last trick, this is really only a fancy way of doing the simple Trick Shuffle described earlier in Shuffle Sorcery.

1 Using this shuffle, you bring the chosen card to the top of the deck.

2 Then you start dealing the cards, one at a time face down, into one pile on the table, at the same time counting them out loud.

3 Ask the spectator to tell you when to stop, as long as it's somewhere before 52!

4 Pick up this pile of cards, put it on top of the deck, and hand it to your friend.

5 Tell him to count out the same number of cards and turn over the last one – it is his card!

6 Let's say he tells you to stop at the number 15. The top card (which is the chosen card, don't forget!) is on the bottom of this pile, so when you put it on top of the deck again, the chosen card is now the fifteenth card. So when your friend takes the deck and counts out the same number in the same way, the chosen card comes out to the top again, and when you turn it over the audience gets the shock of its life!

FUN ON THE MOVE

Games That Travel

Maestro - a little traveling music please! We're going to have fun in motion!

So far, the games in this book have been indoor games. It might seem strange to include car and train games, but not when you realize that you are 'indoors' when you are inside a car or train or school bus. They are just like little houses with wheels!

One thing that is different, though, is that you don't get carsick in the house!

LOOKS LIKE WE GOT US A CONVOY!

123

Carsickness is caused by dizziness from watching the ground near the car rush by or from stuffy air. Roll down the window a bit, and don't do any reading. Look out the front or back windows, where the scenery doesn't seem to rush by so fast.

5 POINTS TO THE ONE WHO SPOTS THE FIRST OUT-OF-GALAXY LICENCE PLATE!!

And while you're looking out the window, you might as well be doing something besides just watching the scenery flash by. Why not try some of the looking-out games in this chapter?

White Line Fever

PLAYERS:
ANY NUMBER

For as long as there have been people, there have been superstitions. Whether or not they are true depends on whether or not you believe in them. Here are a few of the superstitions, new and old, related to traveling and transportation. See how many you can spot in your travels, and keep track of them in a log book. Then, make a list of your own versions of these auto-age superstitions.

1 If you see a white horse, look around to see if you can spot a red-headed person. If you can, then any wish you make will come true.

2 If you see an ambulance, hold your collar until you see a four-legged animal, to avoid bad luck.

3 A few years ago, you could see a lot of cars with three chrome holes in a row along the side. If you see one of these cars when you are with someone, touch something white and say, 'Three holes, touch white, you owe me a dime!'

4 It is generally considered bad luck to speak when you are in a train or car going through a tunnel.

5 It is very lucky to meet a wagon or truck with a load of hay, but unlucky to see the back of a hay wagon.

6 A paddiddle is a one-eyed car or truck, that is, one with only one working headlight, so spotting paddiddles is strictly a nighttime pastime. The first person who spots a paddiddle and says the word 'Paddiddle!' scores a point.

7 Just for the record, it is *very* lucky to collect a million bus tickets, and anyone who is able to do it is liable to be rewarded very generously by the Million Bus Tickets Fairy, a good friend of the Tooth Fairy.

8 When you drive over the railroad tracks, take your feet off the floor, touch the roof with both hands, and make a small wish.

9 When you see a graveyard, don't forget to hold your breath until you are past it. This superstition is older than history.

Telegram

PLAYERS:
2 OR MORE

Keep your eyes on those license plates! If they are the kind with letters on them, you're in luck!

1 Write down the first ten letters you see on license plates.

2 Each player must then make up a 'telegram' message, using those ten letters as the first letter of each word. Letters must be used in the order they were written.

3 For example, let's say that the first ten letters you spot are WWCDBYHTMN. One of the telegrams you make from these letters might go like this:

When Will Charlie Drop By Your House To Make Nitroglycerine? or *We Won't Come Down Because You Have Too Many Nephews.*

4 If you have ever seen a telegram, you will know that sometimes two or three sentences get jammed together without any periods to keep them apart. Sometimes, words like 'a' and 'the' are left out to make the telegram shorter. When you are making your telegram message, it is all right to do the same thing.

The Search Goes On

PLAYERS:
2 OR MORE

Did you ever notice how many stray letters there are along the road? Not the mailable kind, but the alphabetical kind. There are letters on billboards, on road signs and license plates, on storefronts and the sides of barns, on trucks and vans and almost everywhere in between. So with all these stray letters running around, it shouldn't be too hard to play a quick game of The Search Goes On.

1 In this game, each player thinks up any word or phrase that contains eight letters (I love you, my knives, don't stop, et cetera).

2 Then each player races to find the letters in the passing scenery to spell his phrase first.

3 You can take the letters you need from anywhere on any sign, but you *must* find them in the *right order*. Also, if another player spots a certain letter first, no other player can use that letter.

4 For example, let's say you decide to look for the phrase 'I decided.' First you must find a sign with an I on it. The first sign you see says 'Bump ahead.' Oh well, keep looking. The next sign says 'Whispering Pines Motel, 2 mi. straight ahead.' Wow! What luck! Not only does that sign have the *I* you need, but it also has a *D* that you can use! You are well on your way to winning.

Digging for Gold

PLAYERS:
2 OR MORE

1 In this game, the players decide what kind of 'gold' they are going to look for, and the first person to find his gold wins.

2 The gold that you look for doesn't really have to be gold at all. For example, you may decide to look for a crosswalk, a white horse and a train engine, while another player has to keep his eye out for a duck pond, a milk truck and a hitch hiker.

3 The first player to find all three kinds of gold is the winner.

4 If you are choosing your own gold, make sure you don't pick out things that are too easy or too hard to find!

5 If you like, you could write the names of different kinds of gold on slips of paper and choose three out of a hat.

6 Here are some of the many things that make good gold:

- crosswalks
- ambulances
- white or black cars
- special kinds of trucks
- cattle crossing signs

- horses
- drive-ins
- bicycles
- billboards
- postmen

MEET THE AUTHOR

Rudi McToots has had a lot of jobs in his adult life. From chicken plucker to soda jerk, printer, papermaker, cartoonist, animator, illustrator and writer, he has done them all.

But it is his own childhood adventures that make him particularly qualified to write the books in the Adventure Club series. His early interests spanned everything from metal-working and crafts to electronics and chemistry.

At the age of eleven he set up his own homemade laboratory and workshop in the attic and it was there that many of the projects in these books originally took shape – model rockets and airplanes, hot air balloons, costumes, magic tricks, simple radios and telephones and much more.

NOW what's that boy up to?

Brought up in small towns and rural areas across Canada, McToots also pursued many outdoor interests such as Indian crafts and lore, hiking, camping and canoeing.

Today he writes and illustrates books and magazine articles, and works on animated cartoons for major TV shows.

HOLD IT!

Rudi McToots lives in Toronto, Canada, where he and a few friends give writing and illustration workshops in the schools and perform in a group called the Boinks. McToots is the 'human video' as he draws pictures on stage to fit each song.

THE RUDI McTOOTS ADVENTURE CLUB

The old humdrum got you down?

Need a little excitement in your life?

Join the Rudi McToots Adventure Club!

Of course, all members receive official buttons and membership cards.

There's also an Adventure Club Newsletter. Just think – a little adventure through your mailslot 4 times a year.

In it you'll find great articles on breakdancing, making your own videos, sky diving, wind surfing, rock climbing and tons of other exciting stuff.

Like stories of real-life adventures and day-in-the-life accounts of stunt persons, wilderness guides, air-sea rescue personnel, animal trainers, fire fighters and more.

Also, you'll get a sneak preview on the next books in the Rudi McToots Adventure Club series, book reviews, craft and gadget building columns, interviews with adventurers, and news about exciting contests.

The Newsletter also prints stories, drawings and photos sent in by members.

So, what are you waiting for? Fill out the order form, cut, fold, stamp and mail it, and get set for adventure.

ORDER FORM

☐ Yes, I want to be a member of the Rudi McToots Adventure Club.

Enclosed is a check or money order for $7.50 Canadian or $6 US funds, for a year's membership.

NAME

STREET   APT #

CITY   PROVINCE/STATE

POSTAL/ZIP CODE   SIGNATURE

-- Fold --

Name

Address

Postal/Zip Code

Rudi McToots Adventure Club
46 Harbord Street
Toronto Ontario Canada
M5S 1G2

-- Fold --

TAPE OR STAPLE

-- Tape or staple here --